Elizabeth Gartland

The American lady-tailor glove-fitting system of dress making

Elizabeth Gartland

The American lady-tailor glove-fitting system of dress making

ISBN/EAN: 9783337118396

Printed in Europe, USA, Canada, Australia, Japan

Cover: Foto ©Andreas Hilbeck / pixelio.de

More available books at **www.hansebooks.com**

Second Edition.]   [Price, Five Dollars

THE AMERICAN

LADY-TAILOR GLOVE-FITTING SYSTEM

—:OF:—

═DRESS-MAKING,═

Invented and Taught by

MRS. ELIZABETH GARTLAND,

IN HER SCIENTIFIC COLLEGE.

REVISED, ILLUSTRATED & SIMPLIFIED.

PHILADELPHIA, PA.
1884.

IMPORTANT NOTICE.

To ALL WHOM IT MAY CONCERN :—Only those purchasing this Book from me or my authorized agents are hereby licensed to use my Systems of Cutting and Fitting, set forth in this work, the contents of which I have secured by copyright.

And no person shall have any right whatever to sell or teach in any manner, my system, without first procuring from me or my duly authorized agents a license in writing, signed by me, specifying how and in what way it may be used.

MRS. E. GARTLAND,

15 SOUTH 13th STREET, PHILADELPHIA, PA.

LEADING PARIS FASHION MAGAZINES

And *they* can be had at any time by the *single number* or by subscription, post-paid, at the prices given in the following list :

		One Year.	Six Months.	Three Months.	Single Copy.
*Aquarelle Mode	Weekly	$ 16 20	$ 9 00	$ 5 00	45c.
*Album de la Toilette	Semi-Monthly	7 25	4 00	2 25	45c.
*Coquet	Semi-Monthly	9 80	5 50	2 75	45c.
*Elegance Parisienne	Weekly	16 20	9 00	5 00	45c.
*France Elegante	Semi-Monthly	5 20	4 50	2 50	45c.
Journal des Infants	Monthly	5 00	3 00	1 75	45c.
†Journal des Demoiselles	Monthly	4 20			
†Journal des Demoiselles	Semi-Monthly	8 20			
Journal des Demoiselles	Weekly	11 40	5 75	3 00	
*Mode Artistique	Semi-Monthly	7 25	4 00	2 25	45c.
*Mode Illustree	Weekly	9 80	5 00	2 75	
*Mode Universelle	Semi-Monthly	6 10	3 25	1 75	30c.
*Mode de la Saison	Weekly	10 00	5 00	2 75	30c.
Modes Parisiennes	Semi-Monthly	6 10	3 25	1 75	30c.
Modiste Universelle (for millinery)	Monthly	6 20	3 25	2 00	75c.
*Moniteur de la Mode	Weekly	10 60	6 10	3 25	30c.
*Mode Style	Monthly	10 00	5 50	2 75	$1 00
*Printemps	Semi-Monthly	8 10	4 50	2 50	40c.
*Paris Mode	Semi-Monthly	7 20	3 75	2 00	40c.
*Revue de la Mode	Weekly	9 80	5 30	3 00	30c.
*Salon de la Mode, (weekly editon of Printemps)	Weekly	10 60	5 70	3 25	30c.
*Toilettes Mode Illustree, with English descriptions	Monthly	9 00	4 50	3 25	75c.

* These are the very best Journals for Dressmakers.
† No subscriptions taken for less than one year for those marked with a †.

NOTICE!

Our Agents should handle these Magazines, as they will be in great demand, being *months in advance* of American fashion books.

INDEX.

——PRICES.——

One System Book, . . .	$ 5 00
One Tailor's Square,	1 50
One Set of Curvatures, . .	25
One Tape Measure Best	50
One Tracing Wheel, .	50
One Metal Belt, . .	75
One Measure Book, ...	50
One Stamped Pattern of Ladies' Waist and Sleeves, 3 sizes,	25

WHOLESALE PRICE-LIST SENT TO AGENTS.
Instructions Given Through the Mail.

Any of the above articles (excepting paper) sent by mail post-paid on receipt of price. A cheap Tape Line, linen can be sent for 10 cts. and a cheap Tracing Wheel for 25 cents, but neither kept in stock as they are not first-class and do not give satisfaction. They will however be procured for those who wish them.

HOW TO SEND MONEY.

It is best to send the full amount of cash with order as goods are sent by express, C. O. D. unless fully paid for which makes them cost the consignee more. Money may be sent by express, post-office money order, registered letter or draft at our risk (charges for express or exchange on drafts must be prepaid), no goods sent by mail unless so instructed, small amounts may be sent in one or two cent stamps, no stamps of higher denomination than two cents received.

THE SCIENCE OF DRESSMAKING.

To UNDERSTAND fully the Art and Science of CUTTING and FITTING is the most important acquisition of a competent dressmaker; indeed, such knowledge is absolutely necessary to success.

The GLOVE-FITTING LADY TAILOR SYSTEM, as invented and taught practically by Mrs. E. GARTLAND, in her Scientific College, at No. 15 South Thirteenth street, Philadelphia, Pa., is the most *Simple, Certain, Reliable and Perfect System* known, either in this country or in Europe; its simplicity, style and beauty renders it superior to all known methods or systems practised by the best modistes of Paris, Berlin or Vienna, and is peculiarly an American system, and when fully understood no re-fitting or ill-fitting garments will annoy the dressmaker or aggravate her customer.

The many so-called French and English systems are often, as every dressmaker of any experience has often realized, unreliable, defective and deceptive, difficult to comprehend, and uncertain as to the very important matter of a perfect fit.

More work can be accomplished by the GLOVE-FITTING LADY TAILOR SYSTEM, in the same time, than by any other system ever introduced.

The key-note to all successful dressmaking is *good taste*, and good taste depends, to a very great extent, on " what it feeds on;" it is just as susceptible of cultivation and proper direction as any of the other faculties, and cultivation leads directly to method, system, style and taste, and these are the groundwork or foundation of all successful dressmaking.

With a properly cultivated taste, the practical, skillful, methodi cal, systematic dressmaker will rarely fail to please, and this is a very important factor of success.

Taste in style, form, size and color — light and shade — all has their positive effect in producing and developing consistency, symetry and beauty.

Perfection is a very rare thing to be found, — mathematics, we believe, comes nearer to this desideratum than either science or philosophy; hence, by a mathematical rule, we have found the road that leads us directly to the goal of perfection, in the art and science of dressmaking.

Those who study and follow the system and rules laid down in this work will soon be surprised to find how very systematic and simple a matter it is to measure, cut, fit and make a glove-fitting garment on scientific and mathematical principles.

This work is designed to be the alphabet of the beginner — the A B C book to the amatuer dressmaker, as well as the *advisor, director and guide* to those who have had some experience in dressmaking.

Years of perseverance in labor, study, investigation and experience in the vocation of a fashionable, practical and scientific dressmaker have taught us the value of mathematical rules; in this system perfection is as nearly reached as it is possible to hope for or expect.

DRAPING and TRIMMING are matters depending solely on the taste of the dressmaker, — cutting and fitting accurately can only be performed by strict attention to certain mathematical rules, which are clearly laid down in this work; but *draping, trimming and Basteing* are wholly dependent upon taste and good judgment; popularity and success will be the sure and certain reward of those who excel in this respect.

INTRODUCTORY.

THE AMERICAN LADY TAILOR GLOVE-FITTING

SYSTEM OF DRESSMAKING,

INVENTED AND TAUGHT BY

MRS. ELIZABETH GARTLAND,

In her Scientific College, Philadelphia, Pa.

HAVING investigated and studied every so-called self-fitting chart and scale that has been published or used in France, England, Germany and America, for a number of years past, and found " none perfect, no, not one; " we were finally, in self-defence, compelled to think and study over the subject, until our patience was well nigh exhausted; but perseverance is at last rewarded, and we have *invented an entirely new system*, which is based on mathematical and scientific principles. By the use of this system, when thoroughly understood, we guarantee that there will be no time wasted, as in the old-fashioned cutting out, trying on, altering and re-altering of a dress or coat. When the measure is once taken, our lady patron may, if she choose, forget all about her dress, until it is furnished to her in all its beauty and perfection of fit.

We have rules and regulations in our new system for measuring, drafting, tracing, cutting, basting, sewing and finishing. With proper attention to these rules failure is an impossibility. But all who attempt to become professional dressmakers should not expect to stand on a pinnacle of fame, to become a Worth or a Pingat, without carefully studying and gaining a practical knowledge of the art of dressmaking in all its details. A strong desire, a determined will, as well as a natural ability and skilled labor is required of any one who wishes to become an expert. Every one has to make a beginning, however, and the young dressmaker who, with pardonable ambition, wishes to stand at the head of her profession, will be saved many an anxious hour, many an aching head and many a hard-earned dollar by a faithful study of this new system.

Dressmaking requires a very different style of work from plain sewing. There are parts that cannot be done too neatly; there are other parts that must be slighted or a stiff and homely appearance is the result. A lady who is an exquisitely neat seamstress is seldom successful as a professional dressmaker, as it is possible she would be so particular, precise and slow that she would scarcely earn her salt; unless she learns *how* and *where* to slight her work, we would advise her to avoid spending money and time in her endeavors. The information and explanations on this subject alone are worth the price of this book to any one with ordinary intelligence, whether an amateur or one who wishes to become a successful professional dressmaker.

Explanation of System.

Our readers will not be surprised when we inform them that the *armhole* is taken as the centre; having taken the exact measure, by the use of the compass we make a circle of the same circumference. We then commence and from the centre of the circle take the width of the back, which divides the whole body. The remainder will come in as the front. Having thus laid a *foundation*, and commenced in the *right place*, and in the right way, all material under the circle which belongs to the back can be easily tapered into the back, and what belongs to the front can be tapered into the front, and taken up as darts, which will keep your waist in the grain of the cloth, and thus avoid all wrinkles. No proportions are taken in this system, as each part or measure is taken separately, direct from the body. *We fit to the body to give a true fit.* Taking the bust measure to proportion the neck, as some do, is a preposterous idea All persons are not built in the same proportion, some having a large bust and thin neck, whilst others may have a small bust and a thick neck. This system is applicable to any *age, size,* or *style.* If the French style is desired, the body is made to appear tapering and long waisted; the opposite effect is given should the English style be preferred.

As we mentioned before, the measure of the arm gives the circumference of the circle, and we thus obtain a *neat, perfect fitting armhole,* which never needs alterations, whether the person be lean or stout, old or young, man, woman or child of the tenderest age. We give no directions to take a seam in here or there, should the armhole be too large, as is done by other systems we could name. Before closing the shoulder seam the armhole has somewhat the appearance of a horse-shoe. The circle is divided into eight equal parts, and both ends of each diameter is a starting point for some particular measure. When the sleeve is sewed in, be it ever so tight, no complaints are heard of being unable to lift the arms, for they can be moved at will, up and down, right and left, around and around with perfect ease.

THE HISTORY OF THE LADY TAILOR SYSTEM.

Our system differs from anything ever before presented to the public, and we will endeavor to explain it briefly. Were we about to make a dress for a small doll, it is likely that in order to accomplish our task in as short a time as possible, we would do what many have done before us, and that is, we would first cut a hole in the material, and slip the doll's arm in it. We would then taper in the waist, by taking it in under the arms, down the centre of the back, and take in another seam between these two, on each side of the back, curving around to the armhole. We would then take up the darts, and adjust the shoulder seams. Thus it is most likely we would have quite a neat-fitting dress for Miss Dolly. We do much the same thing in our New System. Having discovered that the proper fit of the armhole was of the utmost importance, we spent many a sleepless night in thinking over the subject. We all know if the armhole is too tight, it is sure to tear out, and if too large it is impossible to remedy it.

One cold night in February, when the household had been quietly sleeping for hours, these thoughts, as usual, persistently haunted us. Suddenly an idea came, and not wishing to lose it, we hastily jumped out of bed, crept quietly down stairs for fear of waking the sleepers, and whilst shivering in the cold, we hastily jotted down the first draft of our New American Lady Tailor System, and then returned to our bed satisfied with the results, and knowing we had made *one of the greatest inventions of the age.*

When a physician is called upon to prescribe for a patient, if he first endeavors to discover the *cause* of the symptoms, the remedy is more easily found. Just so it was with us. We were the physician called upon to prescribe for the patient, which in this case was an *ill-fitting dress.* It had a bad fit. We discovered the cause of this severe illness to be in the *armhole,* and we were fortunate enough to find the *remedy* and make a *perfect cure.*

THE PURPOSE OF THIS BOOK.

This book is intended to explain the Principles of Dress-cutting, and is founded on *systematic rules*, by which any one can learn to measure, draft, baste, cut, fit, and make dresses, without further instruction.

To DRESSMAKERS.—It will be of great use to professional dressmakers, who, like the Inventor, have had the same sad experience in the use of all other charts and systems.

To LADIES IN PRIVATE LIFE.—It is specially adapted to the use of those ladies who wish to alter or make their own dresses for home and morning wear. It is as much trouble or more to a dressmaker, to make a chintz or percale dress, as one of more expensive material; yet few ladies are willing to pay as much, for it is probable that the making would often be three times as much as the original cost. If this class of work is done by the ladies themselves, or if they choose to superintend it at home, professional dress-makers will have more time to devote to the finer or more artistic work.

To YOUNG LADIES.—Young ladies, to you this book and the system it teaches will be invaluable. Many of you object to spending at least six or eight months time in learning the trade.

Most of those who do this are but wasting their time. There are few who are taught the art of measuring, drafting, or cutting by rule, basting and fitting, and that all seams are put together differently; some having to be stretched, while others should be held in. In fact, we have known dressmakers who never allowed their apprentices to get a glimpse of these necessary things, but kept them continually employed in one special branch, such as quilling, ruffling, fluting, buttonhole making, overcasting, etc.

The time has now come when a young lady's education will be considered unfinished unless she is an adept in this art.

We guarantee perfect Arm-holes, Sleeves, Bust, Darts, Curves, and Neck without *Refitting.* It is simply perfect in all its *simplicity* and *beauty,* and we are pleased to cut any one *Test Linings,* to *prove its merits.*

Never take instructions in any System without having Test Linings *cut and tried on.* Many claim to be Self-fitting, but judge for yourself whether the fit is good or bad.

We have tried all these so-called Tailor Systems, and do not wonder that experienced dress-makers are disgusted with them. Practice and experience enable us to say that we have yet to record a single failure in the use of our New System.

It is our experience, and the basis of our System, that without a perfect arm-hole it is impossible to have a perfect-fitting waist and sleeve.

Our system is the only one by which a perfect sleeve can be made without a particle of alteration. The rules are so plain, both for measuring and drafting, that with ordinary care a mistake is almost impossible.

Many will enquire, "what is the difference between the LADY TAILOR SYSTEM, or other so-called Tailor Systems?" taught from pasteboard, with imitation square attached which is only a deception and fraud, as no person will ever be able to use a square without the attachment.

By learning the LADY TAILOR SYSTEM, you will be competent to cut like a tailor, by the *tape*-measure alone, designed from any fashion plate, either English, French or American styles. This can be learned in a very short time, a few hours will instruct a dressmaker, without refitting or the use of any pattern.

THE SECRET OF DRESSING WELL.

Good dressing does not consist in wearing costly apparel only. It matters not what may be the cost of any garment, if it is puckered and wrinkled, the form of the wearer will be disfigured and distorted, and she cannot be considered well dressed. On the other hand, we have seen ladies wearing cheaper material, properly used and made to fit with glove-like accuracy, thus displaying to the best advantage the figure with which nature has endowed them, and adding grace to the beautiful, and beauty to the graceful.

It is a woman's duty to have her garments so made that they add to the natural charms of face, figure, age and character, to conceal any defect or deformity that artistic or skilled workmanship can hide. Just here lies the secret of success in dressing well. A good fit makes even a common dress look well, and *to look well is the very acme of beauty in the art of dressing.*

The young lady who wears a dress of expensive material, which is full of great wrinkles on the hips and shoulders and around the neck, too tight or too loose across the bust, too long or too short in the waist, and the shoulders of uneven length, is unavoidably considered *slovenly* by those with whom she comes in contact. She may be a brilliant conversationalist, and a perfect Hebe in face and form, yet the effect is much the same as seeing a mother's big, loose wrinkled stocking upon the beautifully formed limb of a little child, the grace and symetry of which is destroyed, lost and unnoticed.

Cynics may say what they choose, but " *beauty unadorned* " is a thing of the past. How much more pleasant to the eye is it to look at a lady dressed according to the prevailing style of the period, which demands the utmost accuracy of fit and the greatest nicety in making, than to gaze upon the old-fashioned damsel of the backwoods, who has little time or inclination for self-adornment, and thinks of naught but her chickens, cows, pigs, and getting meals ready for the men folks.

Dressmaking is not what it was ten years ago, for within the last few years the tendency of the times has called forth the most artistic skill. The close, skin-like fitting busts and sleeves of to-day require scientific cutting and fitting. A fault at once shows itself, and disfigures the wearer; consequently, it is more essential to ladies to have perfect-fitting garments now than it has been at any previous time. The universal question asked is, "Where can I get a dress made that will not enlarge defects or detract from nature's gifts." A frequent mistake made by dress-makers will be well to note here. How often have we heard it said, "You are crooked; one shoulder is higher than the other." The dressmaker may honestly think she is speaking the truth, but in nine hundred and ninety-nine cases out of a thousand she is slandering one of the most perfect forms created by God and nature. The fault lies in her own work, but occurs so frequently that, naturally, the question arises in her mind, "Why so much deformity among the noblest work of God?"

A NEW SYSTEM.

We claim that our system is *perfectly original* in all its parts, from beginning to end. We cordially and gladly invite one and all, professional as well as amateur, to call and investigate its merits for themselves. It has been faithfully tried, and found most satisfactory in every case. Its simplicity is one of its greatest charms. The directions are so explicit that a child could understand them; therefore, we do not hesitate to invite friend or foe to examine and criticise our work, as we are certain of a decision in our favor.

REPORT OF AN INTERVIEW WITH A PUPIL.

A lady with an intelligent, pleasing countenance, possibly about twenty-five or thirty years of age, was called into the room, not knowing what was required of her. Previous to her entrance we were told that a short time before this, she and her family had met with the loss of the greater part of their fortune. She informed us that as she had several sisters, it was thought best for economy's sake, that one of them should learn dress-making, so that she might be able to cut, fit and make dresses for herself and sisters. She knew absolutely nothing before commencing. We give her own words. "I believe I could thread my needle," she said, laughingly, "but that is near about all I could do; occasionally when I wanted to hurry up things a little, when we had a dress-maker in the house, I was allowed the privilege of sewing on a skirt braid, or stitching up a pocket. I have been under Mrs. Gartland's tuition, on an average about four hours daily, for about four weeks, and in this comparatively short time have learned enough to be trusted to make a whole dress for myself. That is what I am now doing, and I feel more than satisfied with my success; I have most trouble in forming darts, that is, in basting the lines exactly opposite each other. I know I shall overcome this difficulty by experience, as 'practice makes perfect.' I recommend Mrs. Gartland's System cheerfully as well as gratefully to those who, like myself, are determined to learn all they can, to help themselves and others, instead of being a constant dependent on the kindness of relatives and friends." This young lady is considered by Mrs. Gartland perfectly competent to be a professional dress-maker

INTERVIEW WITH ANOTHER PUPIL.

This young girl is employed in the kitchen of a neighboring hotel. Not liking her position, the hours she is off duty, from half-past two until half-past five, she has spent in Mrs. Gartland's Class Rooms, for the last four weeks. She understood plain sewing, and had made a basque for herself, by ripping and taking an old one for a model, before taking instruction. She was all through except making a dress for herself, and expressed herself as delighted with the accomplishment of her wishes in so short a time, and gladly endorses all said by the other pupil.

THE DRESS-MAKER'S CATECHISM.

Every Dress-maker should test herself by the following Questions.

1. Do I honestly consider myself competent to take the goods belonging to another person, and return the garment, when finished, without delay or fault?

2. Do I honestly consider myself perfect in the art of dress-making?

3. Do I thoroughly understand each and all the branches connected with the art of dress-making; namely, Measuring, Drafting, Cutting, Basting, Fitting and Sewing?

4. Do I understand these branches so well that I can finish a dress without refitting?

5. Do I thoroughly understand the new system by which the Sleeve is Measured, Drafted, Cut, Basted, and adjusted properly?

6. Am I competent to arrange the drapery according to the style most becoming to the figure of the wearer?

7. Am I competent to give either the French or English style of fit, according to the wish of the wearer?

8. Am I competent to reproduce patterns or styles from any fashion plate or book?

9. Am I competent to invent new styles without patterns?

10. Can I fit a dress without the aid of Charts of any kind, simply by the use of shears, tape measure and ruler, as taught by " *The Original Lady Tailor System ?*"

If these questions can be truthfully answered, rest assured you have the qualifications necessary to insure success.

WHERE SHALL DRESS-MAKERS LOOK FOR HELP?

Help of all kinds is inferior to what it was formerly, although the salary expected is higher, and the hours shorter. Being an American born citizen we are sorry to be obliged to acknowledge it, but it is our experience that the Germans are more systematic than other nations in the education of their children. The principles of the Kindergarten are carried through all grades of schools, consequently the people are more thorough in everything they undertake.

A number of applicants came to our office in answer to an advertisement. We asked No. 1:—

Ques. " What do you know about Dress-making?"

Ans. " I know a great deal."

Ques. " Could you cut and fit a dress?"

Ans. " I could try."

Ques. " How long have you worked at the trade?"

Ans. " About two months altogether."

Ques. " Can you sew up these seams?"

Ans. " Oh yes; I know I can do that."

The skirt is given her with seams *basted.* When finished we are obliged to give it to another hand to rip, as the stitching is both sides the basting, and by the time the end of the seam is reached, it is fully *half an inch inside* the basting.

INTERVIEW WITH NO. 2.

Ques. " Have you learned the trade regularly?"

Ans. " Yes, Ma'am; I was with Mrs. —— six months."

Ques. " What can you do?"

Ans. " I used to plait the ruffles."

Ques. " Is that all you did in six months?"

Ans. " Most all the time, but I sometimes pulled out basting threads."

She is given ruffles to plait. She commences them one inch apart, and finishes them three inches apart, after six months experience in nothing else.

INTERVIEW WITH NO. 3.

Ques. " Have *you* any experience?"

Ans. " I was with Madam —— one month."

Ques. " Why did you leave?"

Ans. " I got tired of whipping seams and carrying home bundles." The seams given her to overcast were so badly done, no two stitches being the same size, that we did not wonder that her former employer made an errand girl of her.

Is it a matter of surprise that dress-makers get desperate when such specimens as these present themselves for employment? It is true we occasionally meet with better success, but alas! very, very seldom among our own country-women.

Naturally you ask the cause of this trouble. It is this. In the days of our grandmothers, when no such luxury as the sewing-machine was in existence, every girl was taught to sew as soon as she was old enough to hold her needle. In these days even the poorest possess a sewing-machine, so that hand sewing is at a discount, and there are few expert or neat seamstresses to be found unless they are foreigners.

" There are exceptions to all rules," and we would give credit where it is due, for there are American ladies who are skillful in the use of the needle, but we fear they are few in number.

EXPERIENCED APPLICANTS.

We have had applicants for positions from those who have had from ten to fifteen years experience in the old style of dress-making, going around from house to house among their patrons, by the day or week. Having had so much experience, they thought of course they knew all there was to learn, and that it was unnecessary to give them any instruction.

Well, not caring to dispute the matter, we set them to work, and they invariably began in the same way.

They first cut the body lining according to the pattern which they always carry with them.

The lining is so large that two ladies might get in at one time. It is then tried on, wrong side out, and then the endeavor is made to get it small enough, by pinning the seams in tighter. The lady is told to come again next day, and it will be ready to try on again.

The lady arrives next day and finds that the lining had been ripped apart, the outside material cut out, and the whole waist basted together again, but alas! it is too tight in some places, too loose in others.

A WORD TO MOTHER'S.

Mothers, we beg of you, do not shirk the responsibility resting on you, but see to it that your daughters are thoroughly taught to use the needle while they are yet under your control.

The sewing-machine is a wonderful invention for the saving of time and labor; but in order to finish the work neatly and fasten the threads, hand sewing is requisite.

HEALTH OF AMERICAN WOMEN.

The statistics show in the reports of practicing physicians that the health of American women is greatly injured by the too constant use of the sewing-machine. The women of to-day have not the same vigorous constitutions possessed by their grandmothers in the past generation. The style of dress and manner of living may have some influence, but it is probable the sewing-machine has more. Why else do we hear so many comparatively young women, *married* and *single*, complaining of weaknesses of various kinds?

SEWING-MACHINES IN DRESS-MAKING.

The sewing-machine in dress-making should be used only in stitching up seams. The most important and particular part of the sewing is *done by hand*, that is the finishing up. The cut and the fit may be perfect, but if the finishing touches are not what they should be, the dress is unfit to wear.

A STEP IN THE RIGHT DIRECTION.

We rejoice " with exceeding great joy " to hear that hand sewing has been introduced in our Philadelphia Normal School. We yet

hope to hear that this good work commenced in the Kindergarten will
be continued through the Primary, Secondary and Grammar Schools,
so that when our daughters, the mothers and wives of the future, are
ready to graduate from the Normal School, they will know, by theory
and practice in this branch of domestic economy, more, far more, than
most of the mothers and wives of the present.

SCHOOLS FOR DRESS-MAKING.

Dress-making should be taught in the same manner as other things
are taught at school. Pupils should learn their A, B, C's, that is
they should commence in the beginning and go step by step, and rule
by rule, in regular order, and learn everything connected with the
business. Then those ladies who have acquired a theoretical as well
as a practical knowledge in every branch of the art, are qualified to
become professional, artistic dress-makers, should stern necessity com-
pel them to support themselves.

Queen Victoria had a family of nine children, every one of whom
was taught a trade. Why should not we follow that illustrious
example?

To become a dressmaker in high art it is necessary to commence in
the same way as music is taught, that is to learn the rudiments. A
child can soon play a piece of music by air yet know nothing about
music, not even the first letter and in this way never become a musi-
cian. So you can learn to make garments by *Charts* or *Pattern*, yet
know nothing of the art; dressmaking must be taught the same as
music, " by a thorough study of this Book you may become an artist.
Trimming and Draping can easy be done after any Fashion Plate, but
Fitting can never be copied, but must be taught by theory, strictly
follow the rules laid down in the Book and we guarantee you will
never make a failure," Draping can be easily learned by taking a wire
" stand," putting over it a skirt, take any Fashion Plate and several

yards of soft material and drape like diagram as near as possible, and in this way you will soon be able to drape any style you see, and also make original styles. You should devote a few hours every day on this branch. To cultivate taste do not waste your good time by spending six or eight months in what you can learn at home in a very short time in taking a few lessons in theory, Fitting is generally taught in such places by holding the pin-cushion, you might as well take music lessons by holding book while another person plays. There are charts and models which can be learned in a few moments, but after they *are* learned, what do they amount to? Do they not conclusively prove the old saying, namely : " *There is no excellence without labor.*"

Rules for Cutting, Basting and Refitting, see Contents.

TO DRAFT THE MEASURE OF ARM'S-EYE.

The following dimensions will save trouble to any one drafting according to this system, or to any one who is unable to find the height of the circle given by the measure of arm's-eye. The numbers range from the youngest child to the stoutest lady.

6 inches in circumference gives a diameter of $2\frac{1}{4}$ inches.

7	"	"	"	"	$2\frac{1}{4}$	"
8	"	"	"	"	$2\frac{1}{2}$	"
9	"	"	"	"	$2\frac{2}{3}$	"
10	"	"	"	"	$3\frac{1}{6}$	"
11	"	"	"	"	$3\frac{1}{2}$	"
12	"	"	"	"	$3\frac{2}{3}$	"
13	"	"	"	"	$4\frac{1}{6}$	"
14	"	"	"	"	$4\frac{1}{3}$	"
15	"	"	"	"	$4\frac{2}{3}$	"
16	"	"	"	"	$5\frac{1}{16}$ inches.
17	"	"	"	"	$5\frac{1}{3}$	"
18	"	"	"	"	$5\frac{2}{3}$	"

Take particular care and do not get diameter too large. It would be much better to get it the width of a line smaller than larger.

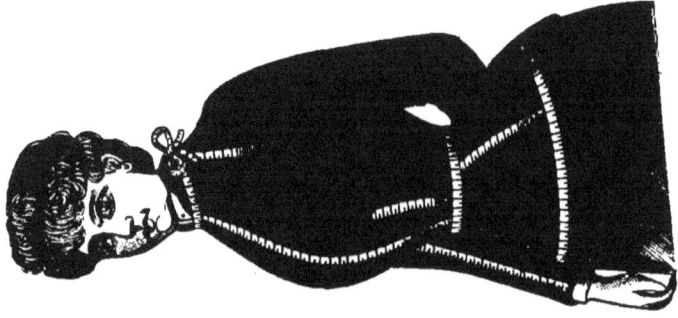

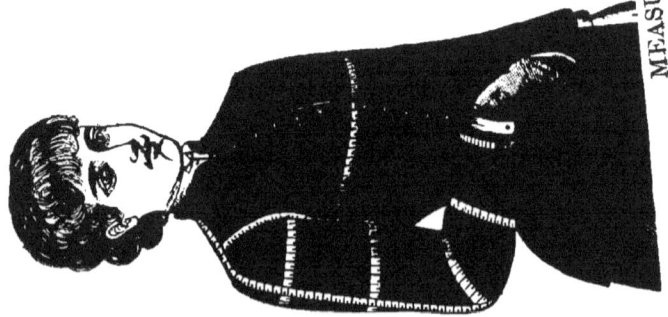

MEASUREMENT POSITIONS. Copyrighted by Elizabeth Garland, Philadelphia.

MEASURES FOR DRAFTING PLAIN BASQUE.

1. Neck, - - - - - - 13 Inches.
2. Arm's eye, - - - - - 14 "
3. Bust, - - - - - - 36 "
4. Waist, - - - - - - 24 "
5. Length of back, - - - - 16 "
6. Under arm, - - - - - 8 "
7. Length of front, - - - - 13 "
8. Height of dart, - - - - 5 "
9. Height of hip, - - - - 5 "
10. Hip, - - - - - - 40 "
11. Width of back, - - - - 13 "
12. Neck to elbow, - - - - 19 "
13. Shoulder, - - - - - 5 "
14. Inside to bend, - - - - 8 "
15. Inside to wrist, - - - - 16 "
16. Upper arm, - - - - 12 "
17. Middle arm, - - - - - 11½ "
18. Elbow, - - - - - 11 "
19. Lower arm, - - - - - 10 "
20. Wrist, - - - - - 8 "

DIRECTIONS FOR TAKING MEASURE.

The tape is taken across the back, very close under the arm, around the front and up over the shoulder · it is then fastened at the side of the neck, as shown in figure.

1.. *Neck.* Take a close measure *outside* of the collar of dress, removing all ties, handkerchiefs, etc., or take a moderately tight measure *inside* of the collar, about as you would have the dress fit.

2. *Width of Armhole.* Take a tight measure, by putting the tape under the arm, up over the shoulder, to the place in which the sleeve is to be sewed. Care must be taken to avoid having this measure too loose.

3. *Bust.* Take a loose measure over the fullest part of the bust, and around the back across the shoulder blades.

4. *Waist.* Take a close measure around the waist. The waistband is fastened around the waist.

5. *Back.* Take the measure across the back, from right to left, on each side above the socket of the arm.

6. *Under-arm.* This measure is invariably taken *too short*, and so causes the dress to tear out whenever a lady desires to raise her arms.

The under-arm measure is taken from the bottom of waistband, close to the tape which is in the axilla, or arm pit.

7. *Length of Back.* Take the measure from bone at back of neck just to the waistband, and not below.

Should a lady be very long waisted in the back, a second measure should be taken from the same point at the neck, down to the extension of her waist, over the waistband. The difference must be added after the first waist line is drawn on draft. This will avoid wrinkles, so often seen between the neck and shoulder blade, and the dress can not fail to fit into the figure in the back, which will also make it more comfortable.

8. *Length of Front.* Take the measure from the hollow of the neck in front down to the *bottom* of waistband.

Should the lady be long waisted in front, a second measure should be taken, and proceed as in the directions for the back.

9. *Dart Measure.* The height of darts is found by measuring from the waist as high as desired. Distance between darts is determined at will.

10. *Hip Measure.* Take measure from waist to the full height of hips, then take the measure around the fullest part of hips.

If a lady has high hips or stomach, or if she wears a bustle, or if, on the contrary, she has small hips or small stomach, and is hollow in the back, note should be taken and allowance made in the right place, and proceed as in rule 27, for Drafting Plain Basque.

. The waist must slope to the back, from the hip to the second measure taken for length of back. By following these directions exactly, we guarantee a perfect fit around the waist and over the hips.

11. *Sleeve Measure.* Place the hand at waist as shown in figure. Then place the tape at the neck, on an even line with the shoulder, and draw it over the shoulder down to elbow, deducting *length of shoulder* desired, after this measure is taken. We then take the measures around the upper arm, halfway between upper arm and elbow, elbow, below the elbow, and the wrist. Also, from inside of arm to bend, and from bend to wrist.

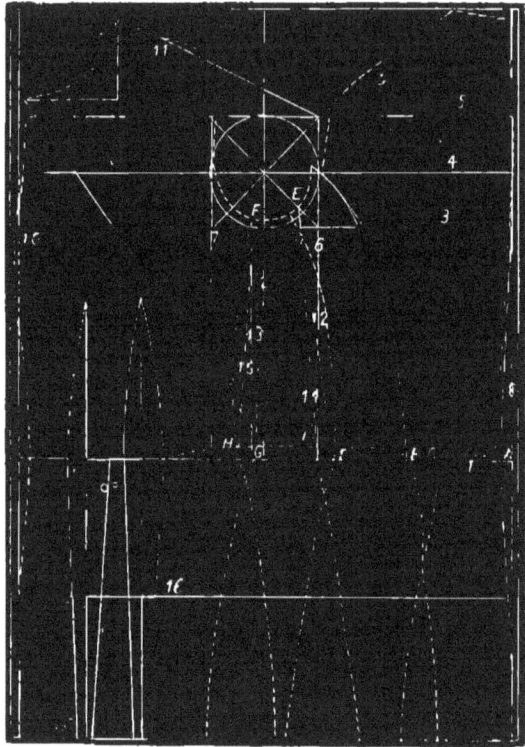

PLAIN BASQUE.

DIRECTIONS FOR DRAFTING PLAIN BASQUE.

1. Draw line 1, ten inches above the bottom of paper, the entire length of square, for *waist line.*

2. Draw line 2 from centre of line 1, according to *length of back.*

3. On line 2 make a dot above the waist line, for the *under-arm measure,* and draw a line parallel to line 1, for line 3.

4. Place centre of circle on line 2, resting on line 3, and *draw a circle according to arm's-eye measure.*

5. Draw line 4 through the centre of circle, the same length as line 3. Also line 5 parallel to line 4, so it will touch the top of circle on line 2.

6. Draw line 6 touching right of circle from line 5 to line 1.

7. Draw line 7 touching left of circle from line 5 to line 1.

8. Draw the slanting diameters of circle.

9. To right of circle, on line 4, take width of back measure.

10. Draw line 8 from waist line up through dot just made, the exact length of back.

11. Dot A is half an inch to left of line 8 on waist line. Draw a line from dot A to junction of lines 4 and 8.

12. Draw a line to left of line 8 for back of neck, which is always one-sixth of neck measure.

13. Line 9 is a slanting line from end of line just drawn to junction of lines 5 and 6. While square is in position, dot for shoulder measure, add one-fourth inch and curve down to line 4.

14. Mark on line 3 the bust measure from line 8 for *front line* of waist, and draw line 10.

15. Draw a line to right of line 10 for front neck, which is always one-fourth of neck measure, then draw a line perpendicular to this of the same length.

16. Draw line 11 from line just drawn to meet line 9 on line 5.

17. Extend line 9 up one-half inch, and slope down to length of back measure.

18. Extend line 11 one-half inch and slope to front neck.

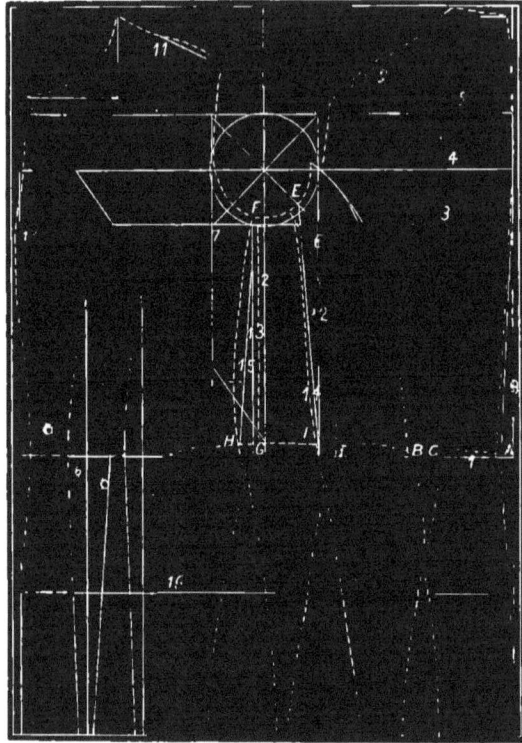

PLAIN BASQUE.

19. Measure space between lines 7 and 10 on waist line; divide space in four equal parts. Two parts in centre mark the space for darts. The space between darts, three-quarters of an inch, is found by placing a mark three-eighths of an inch each side of centre mark.

20 Draw a line in each centre of space for darts; front dart according to measure, back dart one-half inch higher. Then draw the curve for darts.

21. Take half the space between dot A and line 6 and make dot B.

22. One and three-quarter inches to left of A make dot C. Place outside of curvature at circle on line 4, and draw a curved line to C.

23. Draw the curve for side body by placing the inside of Curvature at dot B on waist line, and let it touch back line above line 3, and extend line into Circle one-half inch.

24. Curve the line for armhole from end of extended line, around to touch line 4 on opposite side.

25. Make dot D on waist line, one-half inch to right of line 6.

Make dot E on junction of inside curved line in armhole and slanting line on right, and draw line 12 to dot D on waist line.

26. Make dot F on inside of curved line, three-fourths of an inch to the left of line 2, and draw line 13 straight down to waist line parallel, with line 2, and make dot G.

27. The curve for waist line is made by beginning at back dart and sloping up one-half inch above line 1 to line 2, and down again to back.

28. The curve for inside of side body. Make a dot one-half inch to left of dot E, and use inside of curvature from dot just made to the junction of line 12 and curved waist line.

29. To find the back line of front and width of under-arm gore. Take the sum of the back, side body and front measure at waist line, omitting the width of darts, and mark half the size of waist. Then take half the measure between this mark and back dart and make dot H. The space to left is for front, to the right is for under-arm gore.

30. Draw line 14 from dot E parallel to line 6 and make dot I. Draw line 15 from dots F to H.

31. If the space between lines 13 and 14 is too small for under-arm gore, which is the same size as front from dart to back line on waist line, the difference is divided equally to left of line 13, and right of line 14, and changes the positions of dots G and I.

32. Curve the front from dots F to H; curve under-arm gore from dots F to G and E to I.

33. Make shoulder line from end of perpendicular line at neck, to junction of lines 5 and 6, for line 11.

34. The shortest part of shoulder should be directly on top, and is found by placing point of square at top of perpendicular line of side neck and top of circle, and make a mark at shoulder measure, then curve from shoulder line down to left of circle on line 4.

35. Measure arm's eye, and if too short, add what is wanting to front shoulder, sloping to front neck.

36. Draw line 16 for hip line the height of hip measure below waist line.

37. Extend lines 8 and 10, and slope centre line of darts a little to the back; extend outside dart lines one-quarter inch each side of centre line; to prevent fullness in front of long basque, take out an additional quarter inch to left of centre line of dart, from about one inch above hip line. Uncommonly stout ladies may require two under-arm gores. Mark dots B, C, D, I, G and H on hip line.

38. Slope back line from dot A to bottom of line 8.

Inside of back is sloped from dot C one-half of an inch to left of dot C on hip line.

Back of side body is sloped from B, three-fourths of an inch to right of B on hip line.

Back of under-arm piece is sloped from I, one and a quarter inches to right of I on hip line.

Front of sidebody is sloped from D, one and a quarter inches to left of D on hip line.

Front of under-arm piece is sloped from G, one and a quarter inches to left of G.

Back line of front is sloped from H, one and a half inches to right of H on hip line.

39. If too small after measuring all pieces on line 16, allowance should be made in back seams if a bustle is worn, or in darts and side seams if the lady has a high stomach.

40. The front of waist is curved in from neck about one-quarter of an inch to line 4, curved out one-quarter of an inch, and into height of dart, and into waist line one-half inch, then out to one inch above hip line.

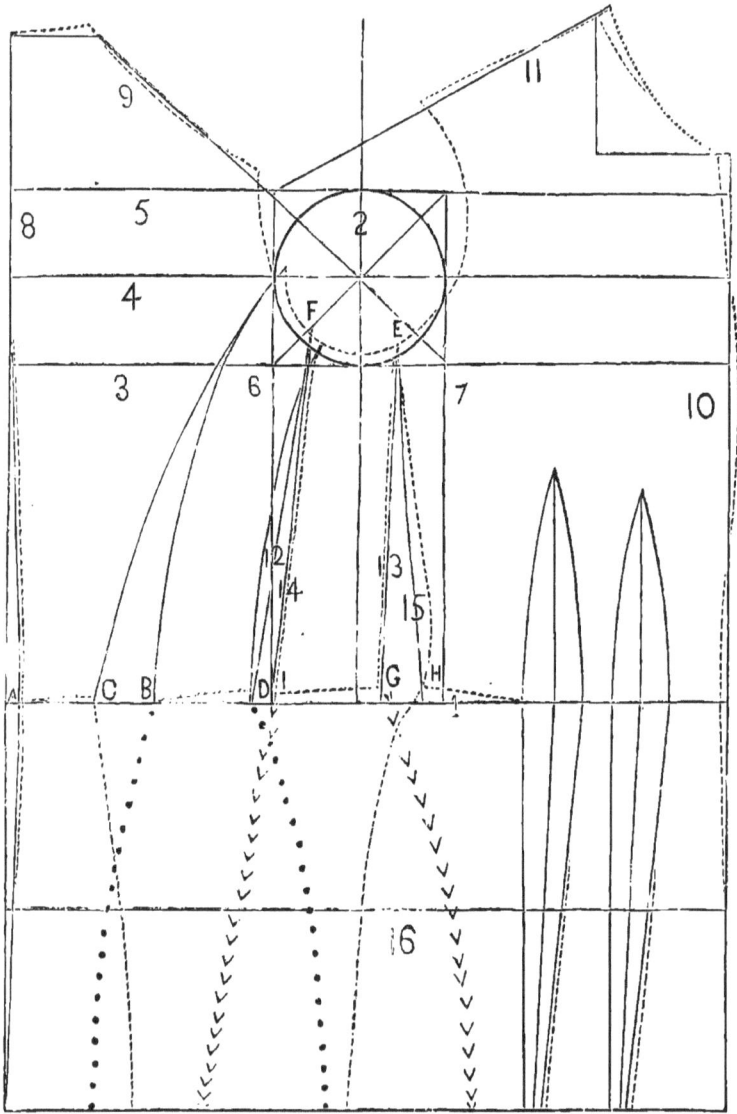

IMPORTANT QUESTIONS FOR PUPILS.

By a thorough study of these questions and answers, the pupil will be enabled to understand the system much better.

Ques. What is line 1 ?

Ans. It is intended for the *waist line.*

Ques. What is line 2 ?

Ans. For the *under-arm measure.*

Ques. What is line 3 ?

Ans. The *bust measure.*

Ques. What is line 4 ?

Ans. The right side of circle is *width of back.* The left side is *width of chest.*

Ques. What is line 5 ?

Ans. The *shoulder line* ends on line 5.

Ques. For what are lines 6 and 7 used ?

Ans. They touch the right and left of circle and divide the body, the back from the front.

Ques. Of what use are the *slanting diameters?*

Ans. The end of the *upper right,* where it touches line 5, is the lower end of shoulder line.

The end of the *lower left* marks the front seam of sleeve.

The end of the *upper left* marks where fulness at top begins.

The end of the *lower right* marks dot E, where inside of *side-body* is drawn to dot D.

Ques. What is line 8 ?

Ans. Length of back measure.

Ques. What is line 9 ?

Ans. Line 9 is *back shoulder* line.

Ques. What is line 10?

Ans. Line 10 is *front line* of waist.

Ques. What is line 11 ?

Ans. Line 11 is *front shoulder* line.

Ques. For what is line 12 used?

Ans. Line 12 is used to find the *front line of side-body,* from dot D to dot E.

Ques. For what is line 13 used ?

Ans. Line 13 is used to find *front line of under-arm* gore from dot F to dot G.

Ques. For what is line 14 used ?

Ans. Line 14 is used to find *back of under-arm gore,* from dot E to dot I.

Ques. For what is line 15 used ?

Ans. Line 15 is used to find *back line* of front, from dot F to dot H.

Ques. For what is line 16 used ?

Ans. Line 16 is used for *hip measure.*

Ques. For what is dot A used ?

Ans. Dot A is on waist line and is used for *slope of back.*

Ques. For what is dot B used ?

Ans. Dot B is on waist line, and marks *back of side-body.*

Ques. For what is dot C used ?

Ans. Dot C is on waist line and marks *front of back.*

Ques. For what is dot D used ?

Ans. Dot D is on waist line and marks *front of side-body.*

Ques. For what is dot E used ?

Ans. Dot E is at the junction of inside curve of circle, and lower right end of diameter, and is the *top of side-body and under-arm gore.*

Ques. For what is dot F used ?

Ans. Dot F is three-fourths of an inch to left of line 2 on circle, and is the *top of front and under-arm gore.*

Ques. For what is dot G used ?

Ans. Dot G is on waist line, and is the *lower front of under-arm gore.*

Ques. For what is dot H used ?

Ans. Dot H is on waist line, and marks the *back edge of front of body.*

Ques. For what is dot I used ?

Ans. Dot I is on waist line, and is the *lower back of under-arm*

☞ALL SHOULD READ THIS.

CAUSE AND EFFECT.   GENERAL INFORMATION.

NOTE.—Those who are ,really desirous of improving themselves, would do well to get a few yards of good drilling, (do not use cheap goods where you are testing anything, as it practically destroys the test), and after measuring some form, cut several linings for the same form, testing the different embellishments and permissible changes which we have suggested in our books. A few cents and hours expended in this way will be of great value and assistance to any one.

THE TRACING WHEEL.

Many ladies purchase the System and learn to use it successfully ; and then, thinking to save two or three minutes of time by cutting out the dress without a tracing wheel, make a miserable failure, and then blame the System for their failure. This is absurd ! Others write for instructions for drafting on the cloth in order to do away with the use of the tracing wheel. It is an easy matter for us to have instructions printed so as to draft on cloth, and to do away with the tracing wheel, but we think to much of the reputation of the System to do any thing so foolish. *The tracing wheel is absolutely necessary !* and should be used in all cases. It *saves* time ; it prevents *inaccuracy,* and it proves the old adage that " what is worth doing at all, is worth doing well." Do not get a double wheel, as it is not practical, and will cause numerous errors. If you are going to cut a gingham dress without lining, and the tracing wheel will not make a visible line to baste by, trace out a lining on thin Manilla paper, baste this lining to your goods, and after dress is all finished you can tear out your paper lining, and at the same time your dress will be seamed up by the mark of wheel, which was plainly visible on the paper lining. Get a good steel tracing wheel and never fail to use it !

PATTERNS AND DRAFTINGS.

In case a lady gets puzzled while trying to learn to make draftings of any garment named in "Instruction Book" or she may have a drafting of such a garment made, and the same traced out on paper, and both drafting and traced pattern mailed to her at the following prices :

Full length Dress, Circular or Dolman   .   . $ 75
Complete Basque, Cloak, Gent's Wrapper or Boy's Garment,   50
Any single part of any Garment,   .   .   .   25

The above prices are for *plain draftings.* Each line is numbered and each dot lettered as they appear in diagrams in books and any lady having such a drafting and traced pattern with the measures to which drafting was made can, with the aid of her book, become perfect in making the same drafting to *any measure.* Any measure may be sent, but in case no measure is sent, the measures in the books will be used.

ALWAYS USE A BELT.

Never take measures without using Belt, as you are likely to take back length too long which will cause wrinkles on the hips and to much length between arm and neck. Strictly observe all rules in the book and we will guarantee a fit without alteration.

The use of Curvatures is to get even lines unless you do this, your seams will not be straight which causes wrinkles. They are a very few who are able to curve without the aid of Curvatures.

Draw straight lines, ...
Curve even seams, ...
Trace in the lines   .   .   .   .   .
Stitch straight, ...
Press seams open   .   .   .   .   .
Rules for cutting and basting, see page Contents.

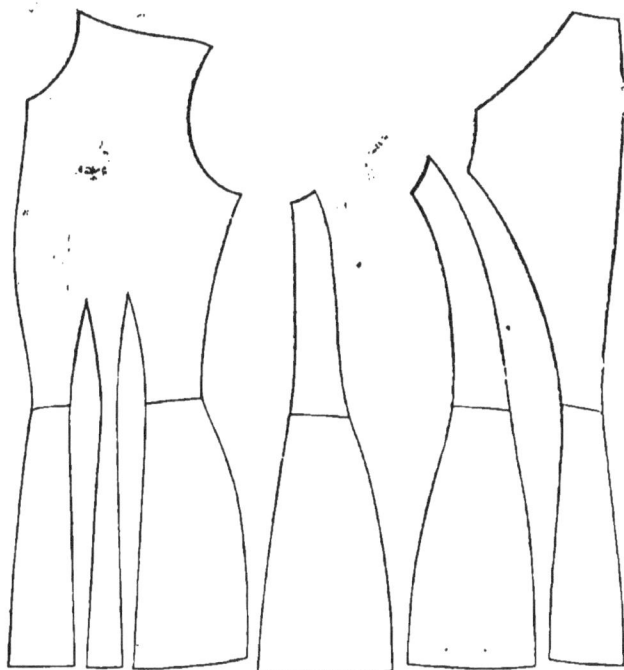

PLAIN BASQUE PATTERN.

Special rules for Measuring and Cuttting.

For Deformed Persons.
" Very Stout "
" Very Slender "
See Contents

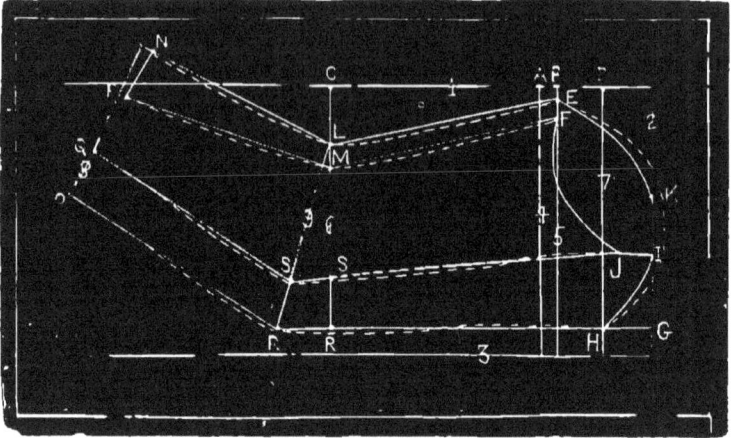

MEASURES FOR DRAFTING SLEEVE.

1. Arm's-eye,	14 inches.		6. Upper Arm,	12 inches.
2. Neck to Elbow	19 "		7. Middle Arm,	11½ "
3. Shoulder,	5 "		8. Elbow,	11 "
4. Inside to Bend,	8 "		9. Lower Arm,	10 "
5. Inside to Wrist,	16 "		10. Wrist,	8 "

RULES FOR DRAFTING SLEEVE.

1. Line 1 is inside measure and diameter of circle added. Dot on this line where diameter of circle begins for A, ½ inch to the right of A mark B. Dot C marks inside to bend measure from dot A. Dot D is half the space between B and end of line 1.

2. Line 2 is ⅔ of arm's-eye measure.

3. Line 3 is the same length as line 1.

4. Draw lines 4, 5, 6, 7, from dots A, B, C, D.

5. On line 5, ½ inch from dot B make dot E and ¾ inch from E make dot F.

6. G is one inch above line 3 on line 2. From G draw a line to line 7 and make dot H. For every inch that the arm's-eye is larger than 14 inches, the space between dot G and line 3 is made ¼ inch larger. In like manner subtract ¼ inch for every inch that the arm's-eye is smaller than 14 inches.

7. I is ⅓ of space between dot G and line 1. From I draw a line to line 7 and make dot J.

8. K is ⅓ the space between dot I and line 1.

9. On line 6 mark dot L 2 inches from dot C. ¾ of inch from dot L make dot M.

10. Draw lines from E to L, and from F to M and from L according to inside to wrist measure one inch above line 1 and make dot N.

11. Place point of square on dot N so the long arm of square touches dot N on line 6 and draw line 8 for wrist ¼ of wrist measure for upper sleeve and make dot O. Two inches to inside of N make P and ¼ of wrist measure from P, mark dot Q for under-sleeve. Take off from the upper and add to under-sleeve if a wider under-sleeve is preferred.

12. On line 6 to inside of dot L mark for elbow, so that the upper sleeve is from 1 to 2 inches wider on the outside than the under-sleeve. Mark R for the upper-sleeve from dot L and S for the under-sleeve from dot M.

13. Then take tape measure and place shoulder measure on dot I and measure for elbow, letting the tape measure pass line 6 between dots R and S and make a mark where your real measure comes to (above or below line 6), then draw line 9 from dot L, passing through mark just made. Then measure again for elbow on line 9 and mark R and S on this line.

14. Draw lines from M to P, from H to R, last made, from R to O from J to S and from S to Q.

15. In curving the upper-sleeve begin at dot E curving up to K and I and down to H. Curve top of under-sleeve from F to J.

16. After curving the inside of upper and under-sleeve measure for middle and lower arm and curve outside of sleeve according to measurements.

17. Extend upper-sleeve from dot N one-half inch and slope down to dot Q.

18. The top of sleeve should always measure at least two inches more than arm's eye. If a raised sleeve is desired, cut the upper-sleeve from one-half to one inch higher.' Dotted line in diagram shows where to increase the curve for high sleeve.

SLEEVE.

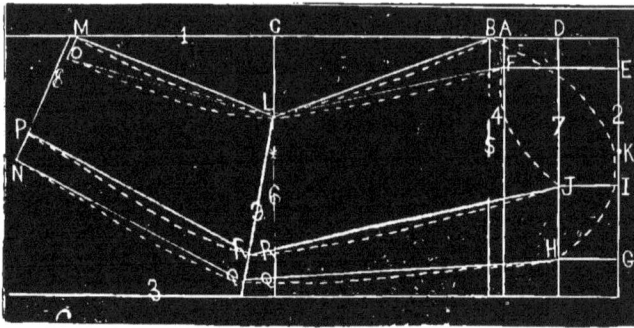

MEASURES FOR DRAFTING SLEEVE.

1. Neck to elbow,   -   -   -   - 19 inches.
2. Shoulder,   -   -   -   -   -   5   "
3. Inside to bend,   -   -   -   - 8   "
4. Inside to wrist,   -   -   -   - 8   "
5. Upper arm,   -   -   -   -   - 12   "
6. Middle arm,   -   -   -   - 11½   "
7. Elbow,   -   -   -   -   -   - 11   "
8. Lower arm,   -   -   -   - 10   "
9. Wrist,   -   -   -   -   -   - 8   "

RULES FOR DRAFTING SLEEVE.

1. Line 1 is inside measure and diameter of circle of arm's eye added.

2. While square is in position make dot A at top end of inside to wrist measure.

3. Make dot B one-half inch to left of A.

4. Make dot C measure from dot A to inside to bend measure.

5. Make dot D one-half the space between dot A and end of line 1.

6. Line 2 forms a right angle with line 1, and is two-thirds of arm's-eye measure.

7. Line 3 is drawn from end of line 2, and is parallel with line 1.

8. Draw lines 4, 5, 6, 7 from dots A B C D parallel with line 2.

9. Make dot E on line 2 one and one-fourth inches from line 1; draw a line parallel to line 1 from dot E to line 4, and make dot F.

10. Make dot G on line 2 one and one-half inches from line 3 draw a line parallel to line 3 from dot G to line 7, and make dot H.

The space between dot G and line 3 is made one-fourth inch larger or smaller for every inch the arm's-eye measure is more or less than 14 inches.

11. Make dot I one-third of space between dot G and line 1; draw a line from dot I to line 7 and make dot J.

12. Make dot K one-fourth of space between dot I and line 1 on line 2.

13. Make dot L 3 inches from line 1 on line 6.

14. Make * one and one-fourth inches to the inside of dot L. The space between dot L and C is made one-third inch larger or smaller for every inch the inside sleeve measure is more or less than 16 inches.

15. Draw lines from B to L, F to L, and from L towards end of line 1, marking dot M according to inside to wrist measure.

16. Place point of square on dot M with long arm touching * on line 6, and draw line 8 from M five-eighths of wrist measure for upper sleeve, and make dot N at end of line.

17. Make dot O one inch inside of M; from O make dot P on line 8 three-eighths of wrist measure for under sleeve.

18. Make dots Q and R, on line 6, so that the upper sleeve be one inch wider than the lower sleeve.

18. To the inside of dot L, make dots Q and R, on line 6, so that he upper sleeve be one inch wider than the lower sleeve for a very slender arm it may be only three quarters of an inch.

19. Then take tape measure and place shoulder measure on dot I, and measure for length of outside measure to elbow, letting the tape measure pass line 6 between dots Q and R, and make a mark to where the real measure comes. Then draw line 9 from line L passing through mark just made, and then measure again for size of elbow on line 9 and mark 9 and R on that line.

20. And then draw lines from P to R last made N to G from G, H, and from R to I and L to O.

21. Extend bottom of upper sleeve three-eighths of an inch from dot M, and draw a line sloping to dot N.

22. The outside curvature can be used for curving the inside of sleeve. In curving top of upper sleeve begin at dot B curving in half inch from dot A, up to dot K and I on line 2 and down to dot H, curve top of under sleeve from F to J, outside of sleeve must be curved according to measurement.

REMARKS. The bend of sleeve can be made less by making the distance between C and L smaller. Can also make the undersleeve one inch narrower on the inside seam. What is thus taken off must be added to the inside of upper sleeve, which throws the seam farther back. It also can be added to the outside of upper sleeve, this will give a little fullness at elbow what some ladies prefer.

N. B. Be very careful in putting in sleeve in the waist, always have outside seam of sleeve touching line 4 in the back in all cases. In basting in sleeve have the sleeve next to you as the sleeve must be fulled slightly, particularly in the upper part of the front of shoulder. Always put cotton in the top of upper sleeve; this will improve the fit. French canvas may also be used instead.

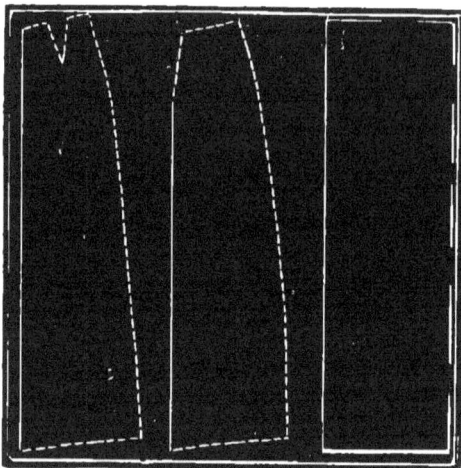

SKIRT.
Copyrighted by Elizabeth Gartland, Philadelphia.

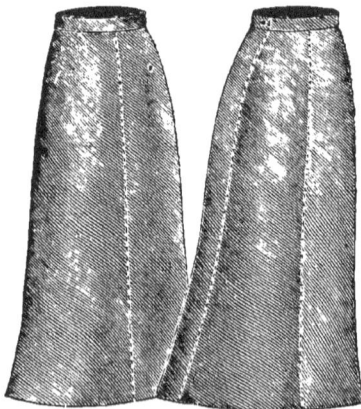

SKIRT.
Copyrighted by Elizabeth Gartland, Philadelphia.

MEASURES FOR DRAFTING GORED SKIRT.

Waist Measure, 24 inches.

Hip Measure, 40 inches.

Length of Front, 40 inches.

Length of Back, 41 inches.

Width of Skirt, 2 yards.

The length of front skirt should be taken, and the darts in top should be shaped according to figure. The side breadth is cut somewhat longer than front breadth, and is but half the width. A dart is also taken off the edge of front breadth, and sloped to fit the figure. The same thing is done to back edge of side breadth. The back breadth is not sloped. In sewing up the breadths, a bias and a straight edge are put together, holding the former toward you.

If the skirt is preferred wider, the extra fullness is invariably put in the back.

Those ladies who like a *long, narrow skirt,* are sometimes annoyed by the skirt catching or drawing in front at the bottom. This is obviated by making two cuts in the front breadth, three inches deep, and about four inches from each side of the centre. To finish off the skirt nicely, the skirt braid should be continued around these cuts. The trimming falling over them, hides them from view.

IMPORTANCE OF HIP MEASURE OF SKIRT.

It is a mistake for any one to think that a skirt is so easily made that no instruction is needed. It is of as much importance for the *skirt to fit the figure,* as it is for the basque to do so. For is it not as impossible for one universal skirt pattern to fit all figures, either slender or stout, as it is to have one sleeve or basque pattern fit all sizes of arms or bodies? A slender young girl of sixteen or eighteen years of age would be lost in a skirt intended for a lady of two hundred pounds weight, or *vice versa,* the fully developed lady of whom we speak would be unable to get into the skirt intended for the young girl.

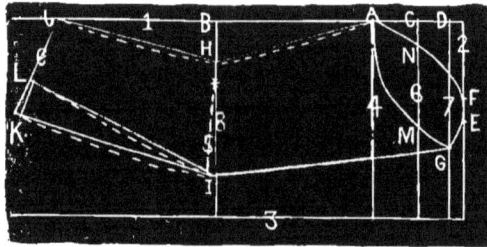

SLEEVE IN ONE PIECE.

This sleeve may be made straight on the thread of the material, but it has a much prettier effect, particularly in plaid goods, and stretches at the elbow like a jersey sleeve when made bias.

Rules for Drafting.

1. Line 1 is inside measure and diameter of circle added; make dot A as usual in other sleeves.

2. Dot B is on line 1 and marks inside to bent measure.

3. Dot C is one-half the space to the right between dot A and the other end of line 1.

4. Dot D is one-third of space between dot C and end of line 1

5. Line 2 is perpendicular to line 1, and is two-thirds the size of arm's-eye.

6. Line 3 is parallel to line 1.

7. Draw lines 4, 5, 6, 7, from dots A, B, C, D, parallel to line 2.

8. Dot E is one-half of line 2. Dot F is one-fourth the space between dot E and end of line 1.

9. Dot G is on line 7, one and one-fourth inches less than one-half of arm's-eye.

10. Dot H is on line 5 two inches inside of dot B. Make a star one inch inside of dot H.

11. Dot I is one-half the elbow measure.

12. Place the shoulder measure on dot F and draw line 8 through the measure to elbow and make dot I on this line.

13. Draw lines from A to II and from II to end of line 1, according to inside measure and make dot G.

14. Place square on star and draw line 9 for wrist, so that the upper sleeve is one and one-half inches wider than the under sleeve at back seam, and make dot K for upper and L for under sleeve.

15. Dot N is on line 6 one-fifth of space between outside line and dot C. Dot M is on the other end of the line and is the same distance between dot C and outside line of sleeve.

16. Draw lines from dot G to dot I on line 8, and from dot I to dots K and L. The upper sleeve is extended one-fourth of an inch and sloped to dot J.

17. The curvature may be used for the lower part of the inside of sleeve, the upper inside and both lower outsides must be curved according to measurements.

18. The top of upper sleeve is curved from dot A through dot N and up to dot F, then to dot E and down to dot G.

19. The under sleeve is curved up from dot A about one-eighth of an inch below line 4, then up through dot M to dot G.

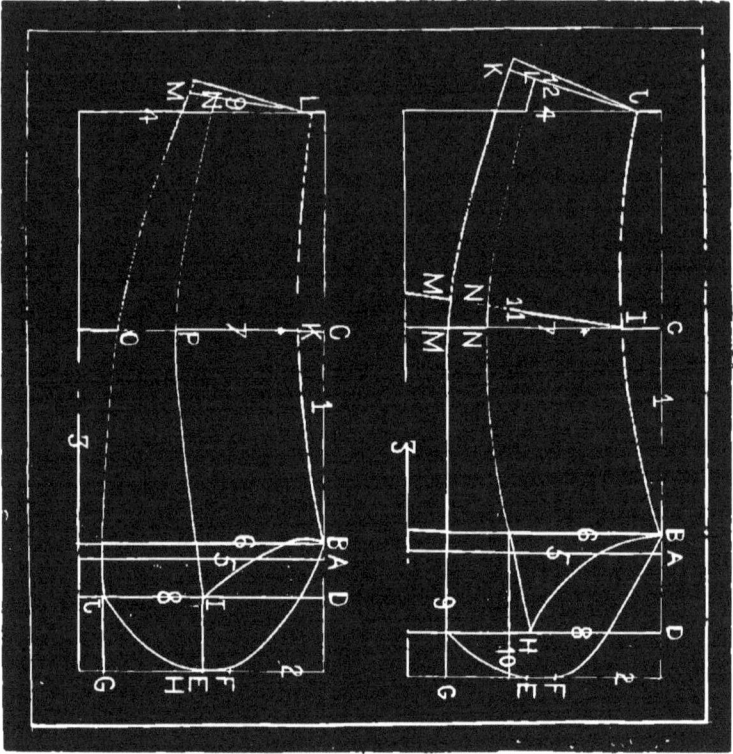

No. 1. COAT SLEEVES. No. 2.

RULES FOR COAT SLEEVE.No. 1.

1. Draw line 1 from inside to wrist measure with diameter of arm's-eye added.

2. Dot A is on line 1 at inside to wrist measure, and dot B is half an inch to the left of dot A.

3. Dot C marks inside to bend measure, from dot B and dot D is one third of space between dot A and end of line 1.

4. Line 2 is two-thirds the size of arm's-eye and perpendicular to line 1.

5. Draw line 3 from end of line 2 parallel to line 1, and line 4 parallel to line 2 from lines 1 and 3.

6. Draw lines from dots A, B, C and D, and make lines 5, 6, 7 and 8.

7. Dot E is in the centre of line 2; dot F is one inch to the left, and dot H is one inch to the right of dot E.

8. Draw a line from dot E to line 8, and make dot I.

9. Dot G is one inch from line 3, allow one-fourth of an inch more or less space for every inch that the arm's-eye is greater or smaller than 14 inches; then draw a line to line 8 from dot G, and make dot J.

10. Make dot K on line 7, one and one-fourth inches from dot C, and make a star one-half inch from dot K.

11. Make dot L on line 4, three-fourths of an inch from line 1.

12. Slope for inside of sleeve from dot B to dot K, and down to dot L.

13. Place point of square on dot L, the long arm touching star and draw line 9 for bottom of sleeve.

14. Make dots M and N on line 9, so that upper sleeve measure will be one inch larger than under sleeve.

15. Make dots O and P on line 7, so that upper sleeve will measure two and one-fourth inches larger at elbow than under sleeve.

16. Slope for outside of upper sleeve from dot J to O and down to dot M, and for under sleeve from dot I to dot P, and down to dot N.

17. Curve for upper part of sleeve from dot B, passing through line 8 three-fourths of an inch from line 1, then through dots F, E and H, down to dot J.

18. Curve for under sleeve from dot I to dot B.

19. Extend the outside line of sleeve one-third of an inch, and then draw a line to dot L for lower part of upper sleeve.

COAT SLEEVE, No. 2.

1. Draw line 1 from inside to wrist measure with diameter of arm's-eye added.

2. Dot A marks diameter of arm's-eye; dot B is half an inch to left of dot A.

3. Dot C marks inside to bend from dot B, and dot D is one-third of distance between dot B and end of line 1.

4. Line 2 is two-thirds of arm's-eye, perpendicular to line 1.

5. Lines 3 and 4 are parallel to lines 1 and 2, as in other diagrams.

6. Draw lines 5, 6, 7 and 8, from dots A, B, C and D.

7. Dot G is one and three-fourths of an inch from line 3 on line 2; allow one-fourth of an inch more or less space for every inch that the arm's eye is greater or smaller than 14 inches.

8. Draw line 9 to line 6.

9. Dot E is one-third of space between dot G and end of line 1.

10. Dot F is one-third of space between dot E and end of line 1.

11. Draw line 10 from dot E to line 6; make dot H on line 8, one inch to left of line 10.

12. Dot I is on line 7, two inches from dot C.

13. Star is one and one-fourth inches from dot I on line 7.

14. Dot J is one and one-fourth inches from line 1 on line 4.

15. Draw lines from dot B to dot I and down to dot J. Place point of square on dot J, the long arm touching star and draw line 12.

16. Mark the wrist measure on line 12, so that the upper sleeve is one inch larger than the under sleeve, and make dots K and L.

17. Make dots M and N on line 7, so that upper will measure one inch larger at elbow than under sleeve.

18. Place the tape measure at shoulder measure on dot E, and mark the neck to elbow measure, passing through dots M and N on line 7. The dots thus made give the true length to elbow.

19. Draw line 11 through dots just made, and mark dots M and N on this line.

20. Slope for outside of upper sleeve from junction of line 9 and 8, to dot M on line 11 and down to dot K, and for under sleeve from dot H, passing the junction of lines 10 and 6 to dot N on line 11, and down dot L.

21. Curve for upper sleeve from dot B, passing through dots F and I on line 2 down to junction of lines 9 and 8.

22. Curve for under sleeve from dot H to dot B.

23. Extend the outside line of upper sleeve at dot K one-third of an inch, and draw a line to dot J for bottom of upper sleeve.

As the under-arm seam is alike in the upper and lower sleeve, material that has to be washed is more easily laundried when made by either of these diagrams.

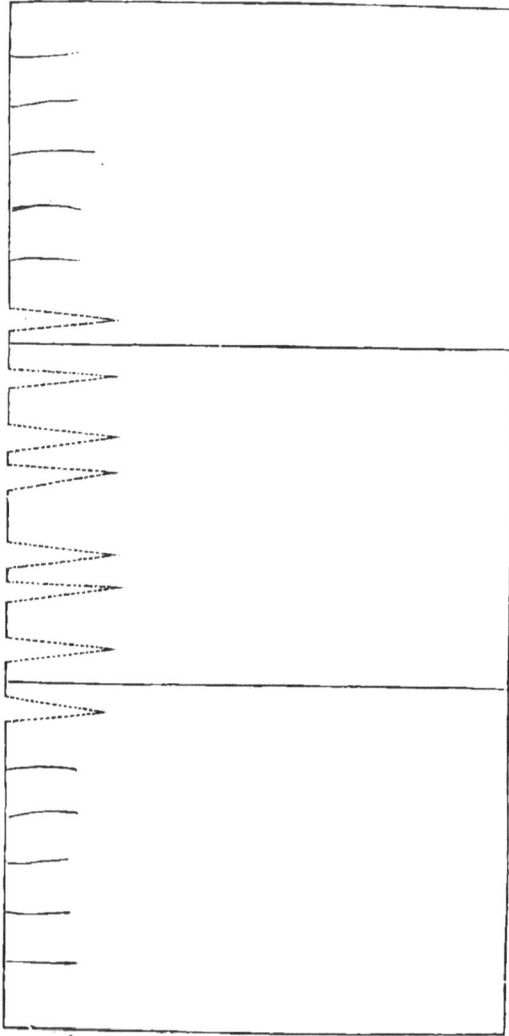

No. 2. SKIRT.

RULES FOR CUTTING STRAIGHT SKIRT.

Sew the breadths together without sloping, until the required width is obtained which is generally from two yards to two and a half according to the figure for an ordinary skirt. Be careful in getting the proper length. Then lay the material on diagram of basque and mark according to measurements of basque below waist line, omiting the back, which is gathered or plaited into the belt without any slope. We thus get a perfect fit around the hips, and the appearance of a princess dress. Trace in the same lines as for basque below waist, take out the same taper between waist and hip line, this give full width of hip measure tapering into the waist without extra pleats, two-thirds of skirt should always be used for front, the balance for the back. If a sham skirt is used baste a piece of material of the same as the dress and take it up with the darts which will always give a nice fit and finish with the appearance of yoke. In making kilt skirt the foundation should always by cut by this rule, No. 2, the kilt plait should only reach to the darts providing, basque is long enough to meet it.

RULES HOW TO KEEP SKIRT BACK.

Divide the skirt in 3ds, $\frac{2}{3}$ belong to front, $\frac{1}{3}$ to back. About 2 inches more than half-way from the bottom of back, sew pieces of tape 2 inches long in even distance to $\frac{1}{3}$ of skirt, the pull-back is passed through the loops and fastened in each end. Rubber or steel may be used, the latter lifts the skirt in the back which requires the skirt to be cut about $\frac{1}{4}$ of a yard wider and 2 to three inches longer in the back.

SKIRT WITH TRAIN.

The dotted lines in diagram are the foundation of skirt; the solid lines are the outlines of princess' dress or wrapper with full train; the short lines are intended for box plaits for princess' dress or wrapper, or may be used for full train.

FULL DRESS SUIT WITH COURT TRAIN.

The train is cut of three widths of material the required length, being square at the end, and is plaited into the waist at back.

When two materials are combined in the dress, as in plate, use the brocade for centre of train.

A breadth or one-half breadth, according to width of silk, is draped around the hips.

When making the collar, before it is turned sew a wire on the edge, or heavy buckram may be used for lining.

FULL DRESS.

Twenty to twenty-five yards of plain silk for this dress, if brocaded as you like in cut, nine yards of each is sufficient.

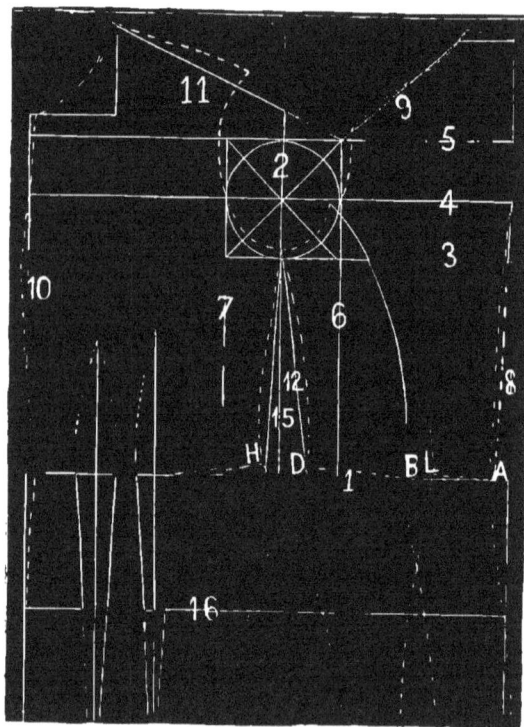

RULES FOR BASQUE No. 2.

This is intended for a slender lady, and has no under-arm gore.

1. Proceed as in plain basque. Find dots B and C as usual. Move dot C as much as you wish the back made wider, consequently move dot B to the left the same distance, in order to keep the space between B and C the same.

2. Use curvature as usual, except that it is moved from one-third to one-half inch below the junction of lines 4 and 6.

3. To find the back line of front and width of under-arm gore. Take the sum of back and front measure at waist line, omitting width of darts, and mark half the size of waist.

4. Half the measure between this mark and back dart, and make dot H the same as for plain basque.

5. Dot D is the same distance to right of H as the waist measure is from B.

6. Draw lines 12 and 15 from dots H and D up to junction of line 2 and inside line of circle.

7. Extend lines 8, 10 and centre line of darts. Mark dots B, C, D and H.

8. Slope back line from dot A to hip line. It may be extended outside of line 8 if necessary.

9. Inside of back is sloped from dot C, three-fourths of an inch to left of dot C on hip line.

10. Back of side body is sloped from B one inch to right of B on hip line.

11. Front of side body is sloped from D two and a quarter inches to left of D on hip line.

12. Back of front is sloped from H two and a half inches to right of H on hip line

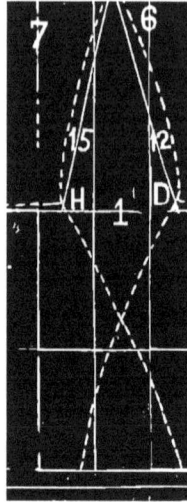

BASQUE, No. 3.

MEASURES FOR BASQUE No. 3.

1. Neck,   -   -   -   -   -   -   12 inches.
2. Arm's eye, -   -   -   -   -   13   "
3. Bust,   -   -   -   -   -   -   34   "
4. Waist, -   -   -   -   -   -   20   "
5. Length of back,   -   -   -   -   15   "
6. Under arm, -   -   -   -   -   7½   "
7. Length of front,   -   -   -   -   12   "
8. Dart,   -   -   -   -   -   -   5   "
9. Height of hip,   -   -   -   -   5   "
10. Hip,   -   -   -   -   -   -   38   "
11. Shoulder,   -   -   -   -   -   4½   "
12. Width of back,   -   -   -   -   11½   "

RULES FOR BASQUE No. 3.

This is also intended for a slender lady. It is in two pieces only, and has but one dart, and an English back.

1. The outside lines are the same as in plain basque.

2. Curve in the back line one-half inch inside of dot A up to where the slope line begins.

3. Dot D is one inch to right of line 6.

4. Dot E is one-half the space between line 2 and slanting diameter on inside line of circle.

5. Draw line 12 from dot E to dot D. Place point of curvature on E and draw curve to D.

6. Curve the front the same as for plain basque, except below waist line, where it is sloped out one-half inch to bottom of basque.

7. From the waist measure take the width of back; the remainder will all be for front. The dart is generally about one

BASQUE No. 4.   BASQUE No. 5.

and a half inches wide, and is placed directly in the centre of front, though it can be wider or narrower, or can be placed farther to the front, if desired.

8. The height of dart is found by taking the difference between the front and back dart, and should slant about one-eighth of an inch to the back.

9. Dot H is the same distance from back of dart as front of dart is from front.

10. Draw line 15 from dot H to dot E.

11. Back line is sloped one inch outside of line 8 on hip line.

12. Inside of back is sloped two and a quarter inches.

13. Back of front is sloped two and a half inches.

14. The dart is sloped one-eighth of an inch to back, the same as above waist line, and may end at hip line or extend in the smallest possible seam to the bottom.

BASQUE No. 4.

Proceed the same as in plain basque; the darts are made as usual; then the back of back dart is drawn one-half to one inch larger. What is taken out in dart is added to the back of front.

BASQUE No. 5.

Proceed the same as in Basque No. 4; then, in order to make darts run into one below waist line, draw front of back dart to centre of space between darts. What is thus added to back dart is taken from front dart at back; then get the centre of front dart and find height of dart the same as in plain basque. Front dart is extended below waist line the same as in plain basque; the front of back dart is extended until it meets the back of front dart about two inches below the waist line.

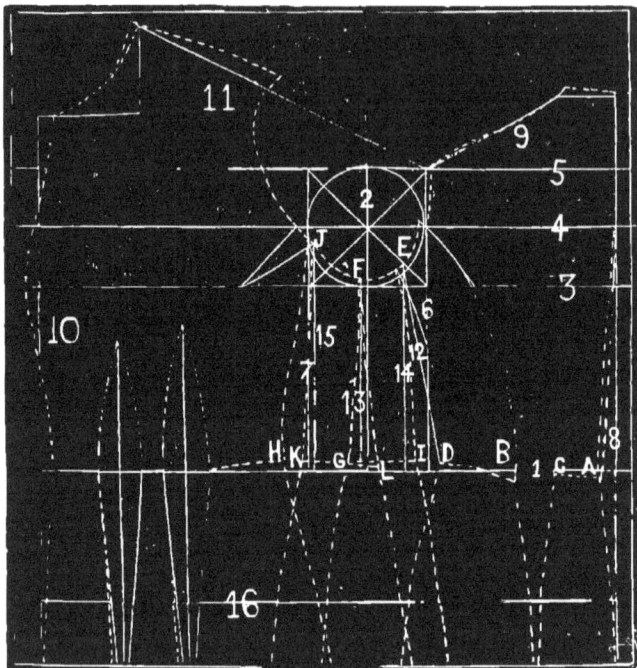

BASQUE No. 6.

MEASURES FOR BASQUE No. 6.

1. Neck,   -   -   -   -   -   - 15 inches.
2. Arms-eye,   -   -   -   -   - 17   "
3. Bust,   -   -   -   -   -   - 50 ' "
4. Waist,   -   -   -   -   - 36   "
5. Length of back, 16½ inches, ½ inch extension.
6. Under arm, -   -   -   -   - 7¼   "
7. Length of front 15 inches, ¼ inch extension.
8. Height of dart,   -   -   -   - 5½   "
9. Height of hip,   -   -   -   - 6   "
10. Hip,   -   -   -   -   -   - 54   "
11. Shoulder,   -   -   -   -   - 6   "
12. Width of back   -   -   -   - 16   "

RULES FOR BASQUE No. 6.

This basque is intended for a stout lady only, and has tw
under-arm gores.

Proceed as in plain basque, not forgetting to add extensions t
back and front, as shown in diagram.

If a greater slope is required in the neck, what is taken off in
front is added to the right of horizontal line at neck, to prevent it
from being too small.

In order to make the waist look more symetrical and bring
the darts forward, the space between lines 7 and 10 is made from
one to two inches smaller; then divide into four equal parts as
usual, allowing a full inch between darts. It is well to use this
rule whenever the space between lines 7 and 10 is over nine inches.

When the bust measure is more than forty inches, a plait of one-
half to one inch and one-half is laid in the front, at arms-eye as
in diagram. The lower line is marked dot J where it touche
inside line of circle.

To find back line of front and width of under-arm gore: dd the back, side-body and front measures on waist line, and mark one half the waist measure as usual. Then divide the space between the back of and back dart and waist measure into three equal parts. Take one part for the front and mark dot H, and take the other two parts for the under-arm gores.

Draw line 14 from E to waist line, and line 15 from J to waist line

Dot F is one-half the distance between dots E and G. Draw line 13 from dot F to waist line. The under-arm gore is then made the same size as space between back of dart and dot H, which is done by dividing the difference in measure, and adding it to each side of space allowed for under-arm gores, and make dots K and L for front gore, and G and I for back gore. For instance, if the space between back dart and dot H is three inches, and the space allowed in draft between lines 13 and 15 for front under-arm gore is but two inches, in order to make the gore three inches wide, add one half of an inch to the left of line 15, and to the right of line 13. The back gore is found in the same manner by adding one half of an inch to the left of line 13 and to the right of line 14.

In measuring the arm's-eye do not neglect to omit the plait, and to add the same amount at top of shoulder.

The extensions below the waist for back and side body are the same as in plain basque.

The under-arm gores have one inch extension to each side. The back of front is extended one inch and a quarter.

If a lady has a high stomach, curve in the darts a little below the waist.

SPECIAL RULES FOR STOUT LADIES.

The back length measure must be taken differently for stout ladies with round shoulders. Take the measure from back of neck to guide, and note the measure. Then from guide to full extent in the waist Ladies of this figure are generally long waisted in the back, and with very large hips.

In making draft this measure must be used up and down on bust line, the same as in measure, as the round shoulder uses up the cloth and will make the dress short waisted in the back, and will also drag the seam towards arm's-eye.

Ladies with flabby or heavy bosom. A tight bust measure must be taken. After draft is drawn, from three-quarters to an inch must be added to top of neck, as the veight of bosom will drag it down.

Also in basting shoulder seam, from one-calf to three-quarters of an inch is taken up beyond tracing line on front, from neck to arm's-eye A lady of this figure likes the feeling of a tight dress.

The darts in front must be thrown back a trifle, perhaps a half to three-quarters of an inch more than for a slender fiigure; a little more curve is required between height of dart and waist line.

SPECIAL RULES FOR SLENDER LADIES.

Slender ladies with round shoulders. The length of back is taken the same as for stout ladies.

Fewer seams, greater space in back and between darts give a less slender appearance.

An English back should be worn by a very slender lady.

One of the advantages of this system is that the seams and spaces can be made to suit both *wearer* and *cutter,* and never interfere with the fit of dress.

To give a square shoulder, cut the shoulder one-half inch to 1 inch longer and put three or four layers of cotton between outside and lining. In putting in the sleeve, put it over the waist as short as you wish the shoulder to be, do not cut the waist under the sleeve, put the extra fullness on top of sleeve this will give a square shoulder, the inside of waist may be boded like cut of Riding Habit waist.

To give the appearance of a square shoulder cut the shoulder a trifle longer and put three or for layers of cotton between outside and lining. In putting in the sleeve put it over the waist as short as you wish the shoulder to be

Do not cut the waist under the sleeve, and put extra fullness on top of sleeve. This will give a square shoulder. The inside of waist may be padded like cut of Riding Habit shows.

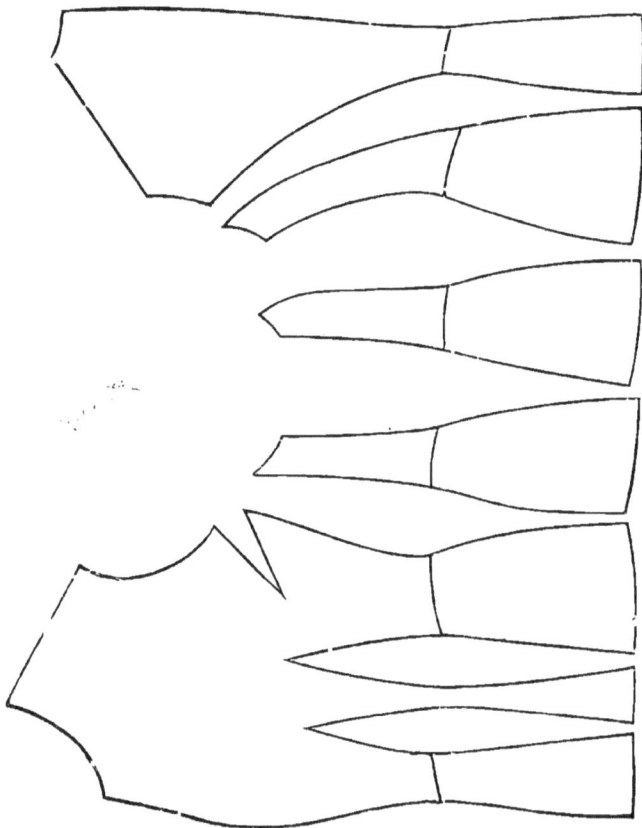

STOUT LADY'S WAIST PATTERN.

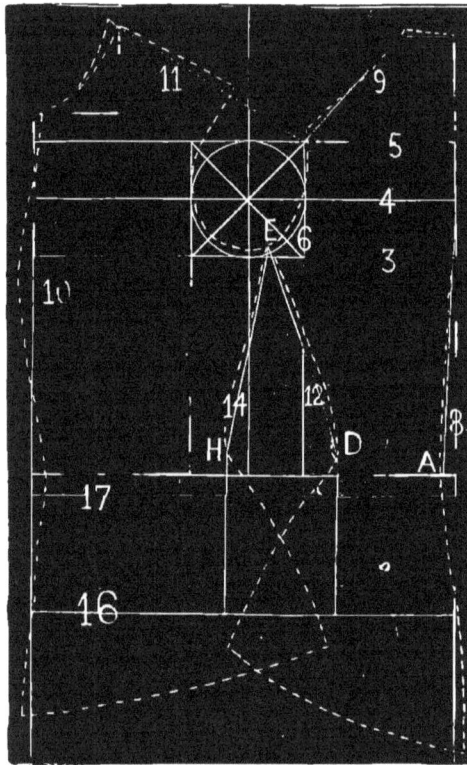

STOCKINET JERSEY WAIST.

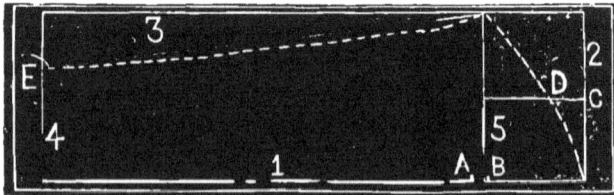

SLEEVE.

STOCKINET JERSEY WAIST.

This is cut on the same principle as basque No. 3, with English back and no under-arm gore, except that it is usual to omit the dart.

Make the draft from two to four inches less than actual measurement of waist and bust, according to the elasticity of the goods. To prevent the waist from being short waisted, add one inch to length of back, one-half at top of neck and one-half below the waist line; to the front add one inch below the waist line, also in front curve in one inch at waist.

When no darts are used, all the cloth should be taken out at the side as shown in diagram. The under-arm seam must be one inch shorter than measure to waist line, and the skirt below the waist line is four inches shorter than front skirt. This prevents the bias seam from stretching longer than front or back.

One length of full width stockinet jersey cloth, or in other words three-fourths of a yard is all that is required for making a medium sized house jersey.

DIRECTIONS FOR DRAFTING STOCKINET
JERSEY SLEEVE.

1. Draw line 1 the length of inside wrist measure and diameter of circle added.

2. Dot on this line for it, where diameter of circle begins. Dot B is one-half inch to right of A.

3. Line 2 is one-half of upper-arm measure.

4. Line 3 is the same length as line one.

5. Line 4 is drawn from end of line 1 to line 3.

6. Line 5 from dot B to line 3.

7. Dot C marks one-half of line 2. Draw a line from C to line 5.

8. Dot D is one-third of line just drawn.

9. Dot E is one-half of wrist measure from line 1.

10. Draw a line from junction of line 3 and 5 to dot E and curve this line in about a quarter of an inch.

11. Curve top of sleeve from junction of line 3 and 5 through dot D to junction of lines 1 and 2.

By cutting this sleeve lay the material double on line 1 and cut around the pattern. The sleeve is put in the waist so the inside seam meets line 2.

BASQUE, with Plaits in Back.

DIRECTIONS FOR MAKING PLAITS IN BACK OF BASQUE.

If the lady is short-waisted an addition of about five inches is made at Waist line, on each side of back ; when the Basque is put together this forms a double box plait on each side of the back seam. If the lady is long-waisted the addition is made at the extension of back, one or two inches below waist.

Make four or five inches on each side of back form according to the fullness desired. If a lady is short-waisted this addition is made one or two inches below Waist line, which will give her the appearance of a long waist. To give a short-waisted effect start at the Waist line. The plaits are continued for Princess Dress or Wrapper.

POLANAISE, PRINCESS DRESS AND WRAPPER.

These are all cut on the same principle as the Plain Basque. They may have either one or two darts, which are carried below waist to hip. Prepare the pattern the same as for Basque. Cut each part of lining first, and lay front and under-arm on material, letting the front side-body touch on hip measure. Keep the pattern straight on waist line, without cutting open, then cut down the full length of skirt. Always lay the pattern so as to slope out in front, about an inch and a half or two inches below the hip line. By thus sloping wider it will meet at the bottom of skirt, and always keep the dress from riding up in front.

The *Waist Lining* should reach to about eight inches below waist, if not lined all through, so as to take up a plait below the hip, behind the front side-body, which will always keep your skirt from throwing unnecessary fullness toward the front. This is done on draft before the pattern is traced on lining.

These garments may all be cut with or without plaits or train. The dotted lines in back of pattern are intended for box plaits.

A long or short coat, an ulster and a polonaise, are also cut on the same principle. The last named may be draped according to taste.

The *back of same dress.* Lay your lining or paper pattern on goods the same as front. If double width goods is used, lay the centre of back on fold, with the lining or pattern about six or seven inches from the edge of back.

The *back side-body* is placed the same distance from the back form as the back is from the edge, which will allow for fullness in the back.

Cut around the pattern of waist, leaving the cloth in one piece about one-half yard longer than skirt measure below waist, which will make the drapery of polonaise.

PRINCESS DRESS COAT & WRAPPER

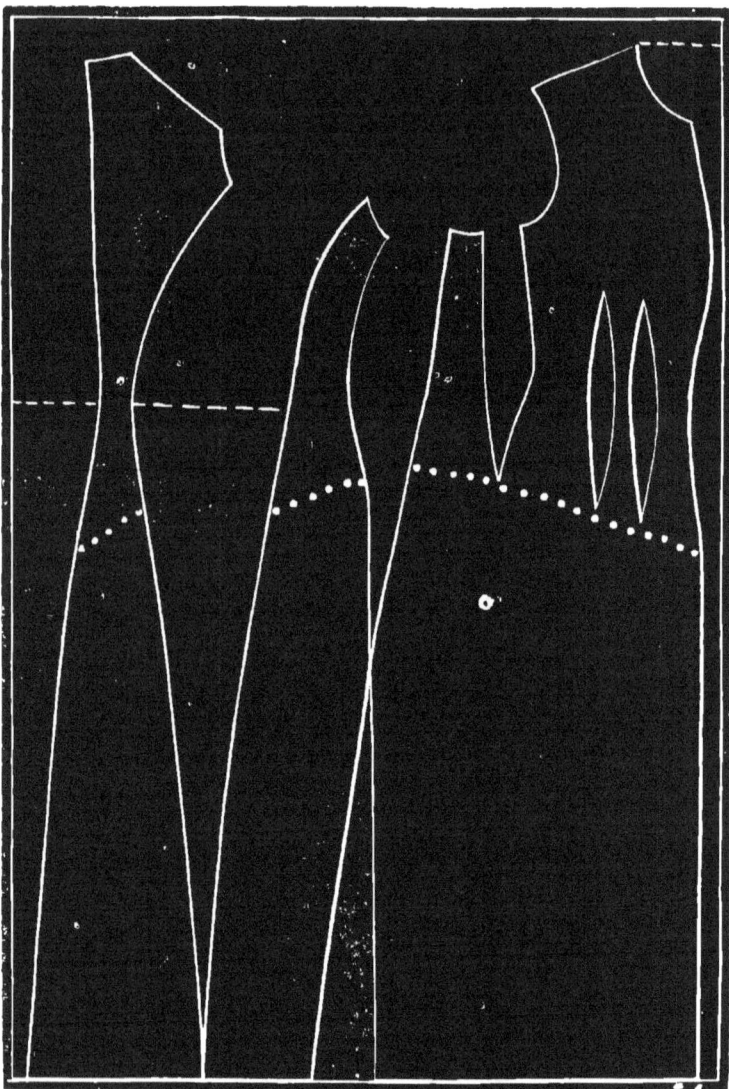

PRINCESS DRESS OR WRAPPER.

ULSTER WITH CAPE.

This is cut the same as the plain ulster. The cape is cut by draft like a yoke, except that it is deeper, there should be no seam in the back.

The shoulder pieces are cut a little wider and higher than upper sleeve.

FRONT and BACK OF SEALSKIN & SEAL PLUSH COAT.

This is cut in the same plan as basque No. 2, in three pieces with or without dart, coat sleeve with cuff rolling collar. Double the length of material, fifty-six inches wide is sufficient for this coat.

CUTAWAY.

WALKING JACKET.

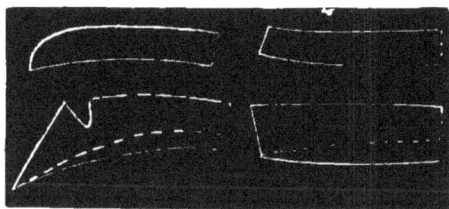

COLLARS.

QUANTITY OF MATERIAL REQUIRED.

Basque for Slender Lady.

Material, 24 inches wide,   -   -   -   3 yards.
Extra for plaits in back,   -   -   -   0¼   "
Silesia for lining,   -   -   -   -   2   "

Basque for Stout Lady.

Material, 24 inches wide,   -   -   3½ to 4½ yards.
Lining   -   -   -   -   -   -   2¼   "

Princess Dress and Wrapper.

Material, 24 inches wide,   -   -   6 to 7 yards
   "   48   "   "   -   -   -   3½   "
Lining,   -   -   -   -   -   -   2   "

Extra allowance must be made for plait in back and train.

Ulster and Coat.

Twice the length of garment, measured from shoulder to length required is sufficient when the cloth is one and one-half, to two yards in width. A lady's long coat, medium size will take six and one-half yards of material, 24 inches wide.

Polonaise.

Material, 24 inches wide,   -   -   7 to 8 yards.

Plain Skirt without Gores.

Material, 24 inches wide,   -   -   -   5 yards.
   "   48   "   "   -   -   -   2½   "

If tucks are desired, allowance must be made for extra material.

Gored Skirt.

Material, 24 inches wide,	-	-	-	4½ yards.
Extra for trimming,	-	- -	-	1 to 2 "
Material, 48 inches wide,	-	-	-	2½ "
Extra for trimming,	-	-	-	0¾ to 1 "

Child's Suit.

Material 24 inches wide, 6 to 7 yards required for a child 6 years old. One to one and a half yards more for each additional year.

Boy's Suit.

Material for jacket, 2 yards of single width for boy of six years; half the quantity for double-width goods.

Material for pants, 1¼ yards for single-width and the length of pants in double-width goods.

Allow one-quarter to one-half of a yard more material in jacket for every additional year.

Dolman.

Material 22 inches wide,	-	-	-	9 yards.
" 48 " "	-	-	- ,	4¼ "
" 54 " "	-	-	-	4 "

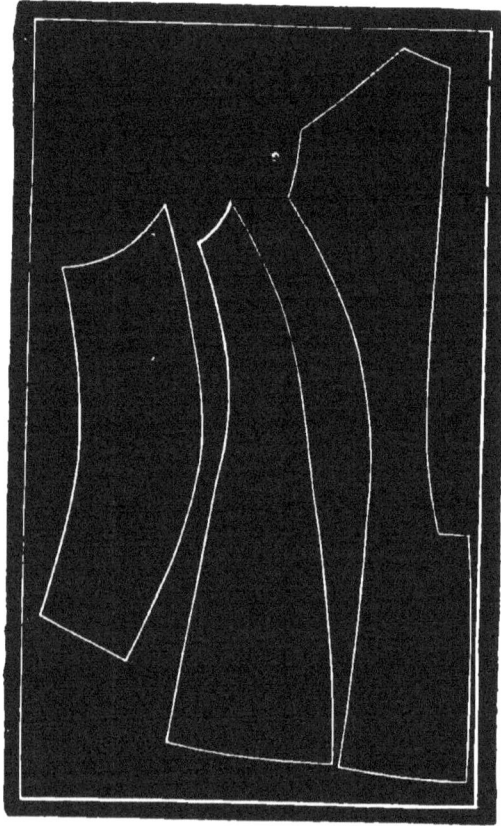

BACK OF TAILOR CUT COAT.

To make new market or ulster, cut down the full length of dress skirt, front view on opposite page, is done in the same moment can be made single or double-brested, this pattern is for short coat.

FRONT PATTERN DOUBLE-BREASTED COAT.

This diagram is so easily drawn that little extra instruction is needed. The double-breasted effect is made by doubling the material over at front line the required width, and shaping the lap as in diagram. The *diagonal front* is made in the same manner. When a tight fitting coat or waist is desired a seam is taken in according to the curve of the front line.

When one dart is used as in this coat, it may be curved around us in diagram and a pocket inserted.

This dress is cut plain Gabriel or in other words Princess, with plaiting at the bottom with a straight piece gathered and turned up which
forms a puff with a cutaway coat like dotted line in diagram opposite.

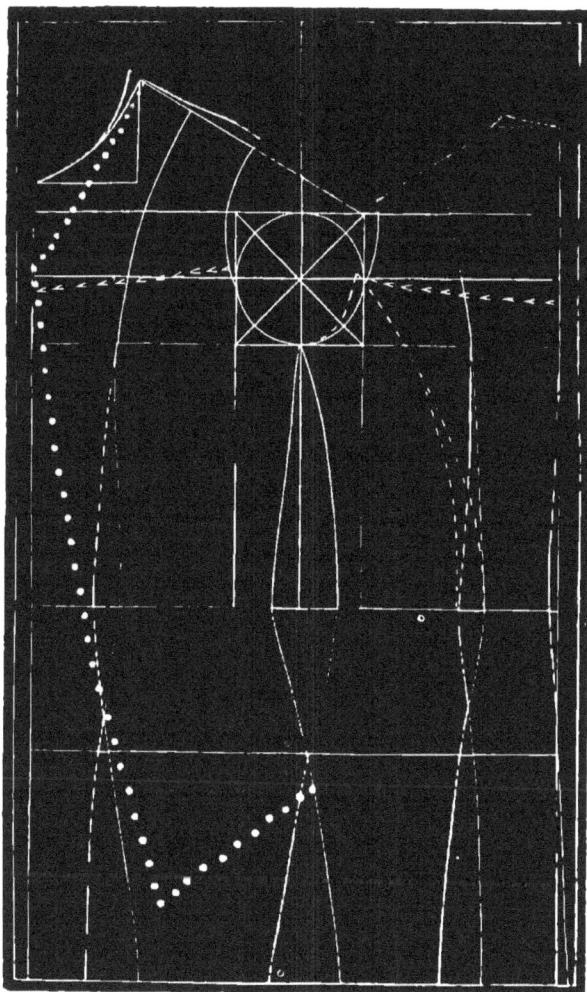

CHILD'S DRESS.

CHILD'S DRESS.

This is drafted on the same principle as plain basque for lady. The measures are taken in the same manner. No darts are required in a child's dress, but one dart may be used in a dress for a miss.

The diagram shows how the draft may be drawn, either plain, with or without yoke, side-body or seam to shoulder. It may also be made with a vest, or a cutaway, and may be trimmed according to taste.

The skirt is also cut the same as that of a Lady's.

For Mother Hubbard the yoke which you see in Diagram marked thus > > > > > is used with a straight piece of material gathered on, completes this dress.

For Gabrielle dress straight lines in diagram are used.

The same lines for basque any length desired.

If buttoned in back allow for lap in cutting lining. Dots in diagram indicate cut-away. Blou. waists are made the same as directions given for gymnastic suits.

Measures for children are taken the same as for ladies, only not so tight.

A child's dress must be loose to be stylish. Aprons are cut on the same principles.

BATHING SUIT.

MOTHER HUBBARD WRAPPER.

This garment can be cut by the opposite plan of bathing suit draft with extra cloth added to the back and front for gathers which are continued the full length of skirt desired, follow the same rule for children.

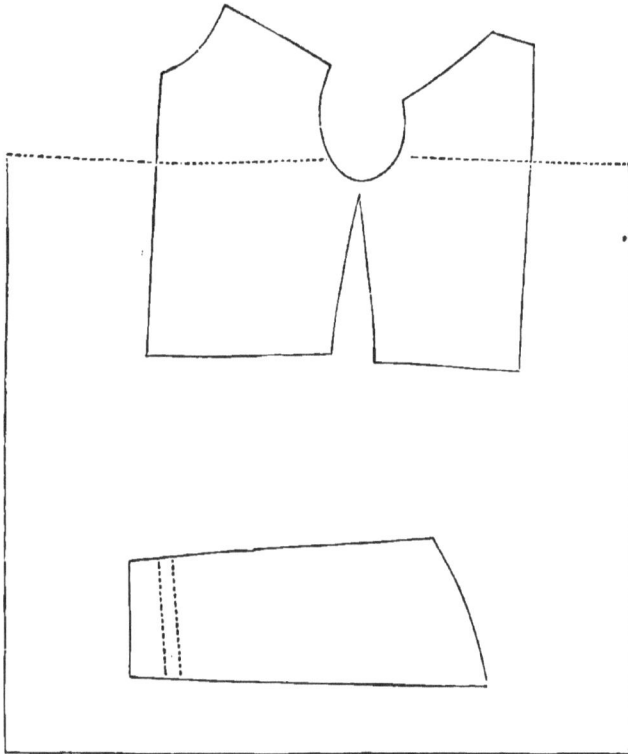

BATHING SUIT DRAFT.

BATHING SUIT.

If a plain bathing suit is needed, draw the yoke from draft, and add about five inches to the back of yoke, and seven inches to the front before cutting the waist, as shown in the diagram; continue down below the waist line for full length of skirt, if the suit is to be all in one; if preferred, the skirt may be separate, and gored as in plate.

It seems scarcely necessary to add that, when cut according to diagram, the lower part of waist should be separated from yoke, and gathered or plaited into it. A leather belt or one made of the material may be worn.

The drawers may be drafted the same as in boy's suit, or they may be cut six to eight inches wider at the bottom, and gathered in at or above the ankle, as shown in the plate.

The sleeve is a regular coat sleeve, or it may be made wider and gathered into the wrist to correspond with the bottom of pants.

In making this suit, about four yards of double-width material is required. It is generally made of flannel for woollen goods of some kind, as the body feels less chilled by contact when wet.

In Europe a sort of twilled cotton goods, similar to drilling or ticking, is used; it is made in red, blue or yellow, striped with white, or some contrasting color, and trimmed with knit lace to match. This material is softt and pleasant to the touch, and yet heavy enough not to cling to the person after bathing.

LAWN-TENNIS SUIT.

The skirt of this suit is made of lady's cloth, flannel or striped stockinet in two or more bright colors, and requires four lengths of single-width material.

The waist may be made similar to the blouse of the gymnastic suit, but a dark jersey waist, matching one of the colors in the skirt, is often worn.

BAPTISMAL ROBES.

Are made of black or white flannel, serge, cashmere, or merino, in the severest and plainest style. They may be cut according to diagram for bathing suit; it is usual to put lead into the hem of the skirt to prevent it from flouting.

YOUNG GIRL'S GRADUATING DRESSES.

Are made of white or cream colored nun's veiling, or of very sheer organdie. They are made in the simplest style, usually with a round waist fulled into an embroidered yoke. The skirt and apron drapery are trimmed with ruffles, edged with Valenciennes lace.

Confirmation suits should have little or no trimming on them, and should be made of white nun's veiling, victoria lawn or any plain white goods that is not too sheer. The high neck and long sleeve should be lined. The skirt is usually plain, and tucked nearly to the waist.

The Roman Catholic candidates for confirmation wear a long silk illusion veil ; a long ribbon sash is worn around the waist, tied in a bow, and hangs down at the side.

GYMNASTIC SUIT.

This suit is generally made of flannel or lady's cloth, and requires four yards of double-width, or eight yards of single-width material.

The blouse is cut by the outside lines of draft for plain waist, adding one inch to length of shoulder, and two inches to bust measure; divide the extra fullness between the back and front, which will cause the draft to be one-half inch wider each side of arm's-eye; the belt should not be too tight, and it should be about three inches wide. As the blouse hangs over the belt, when finished, it should be cut fully nine or ten inches longer than to waist line. Allowance should be made for a wide box plait each side of back and front.

The skirt should be four yards wide, and just long enough to cover the knees; allowance should be made for a hem three inches deep; it is then plaited into the belt in four double box plaits,—one in front, another at the back, and one on each hip.

The sleeve is in one piece, and is fully eighteen or twenty inches wide; it is sloped off at the top about two inches, and inside of arm about one and a half inches. Allowance should be made for a ruffle and facing before cutting out the sleeve; a casing is run into the goods at the head of the facing, and if an elastic is put into it, the bottom of the sleeve forms a ruffle.

The pants are twenty-two inches wide at the bottom, and are similar to the bathing pants,—they are finished up, the same as the sleeve, with a ruffle; they should be long enough to reach below the knee, but they are generally brought above it, and hang over just as the blouse does; they should not be visible below the skirt; the stockings should always match in color.

LONG DOLMAN.

This can be made with or without plaits according to taste, 6 yards of single width or double width 54 inches, 2 width from the shoulder down the skirt desired is sufficient

DOLMAN DRAFT.

MEASURES FOR DOLMAN.

The measures for dolman are taken the same as in ordinary basque, except the sleeve, of which there are three measures, viz :—

First measure,   -   -   -   -   20½ inches.
Second   "   -   -   -   -   -   22   "
Third   "   -   -   -   -   -   21   "

1. Place the hand at waist, then measure from the middle of back, straight across the centre of arms-eye to middle of front.

2. Measure across the fullest part of bust, from back line to front line, over the outside of arm.

3. Measure from centre of back, on a line with the elbow, around the outside of arm to wrist bone.

RULES FOR DRAFTING DOLMAN.

1. Draft outside lines as in plain basque; make dots B and C as in ordinary basque, and move dot B as far to the left as dot C is moved from its usual place.

2. Three inches from dot A make dot C. The back at waist line can be made wider, if preferred.

3. Slope down from shoulder measure to line 3, about one-third the distance between lines 6 and 8, continue down to dot C.

4. Front of dolman. Slope down from shoulder measure to line 3 about one inch to left of line 7. The curve is continued down to dart on hip, and then across to dot B a little above hip line.

5. The dart is made three-fourths of an inch each side of line 2, and is sloped down to hip line.

6. The sleeve commences where the shoulder line touches line 2, and curves down each side, touching the top corners of square formed on arms-eye. The back slopes down to dot C, parallel

with curved line of back. The front is sloped down according to measures. Any style of sleeve may be used according to taste.

7. The extensions are made to allow four inches more than hip measure.

S. Plaits in back are done the same as the postillion basque.

Use same measure and draft by the rule as boy's pants, width for gather may be added as much extra as would be desired according to taste, if bloomers are desired follow the rule of bathing suit pants.

SHORT DOLMAN.

This is cut in same plan as the long one, may be trimmed according to taste with lace or fringe, a skirt garment of this style requires plenty trimmings from 2½ to 3 yards of silk, velvet or plush single width is sufficient.

RUSSIAN CIRCULAR.

This must be cut with from 3 to 6 inches extension on each side of back form commencing about 2 inches below waist line, must be from $2\frac{3}{4}$ to 3 yards wide at the bottom when finished, can be lined with quilted silk or satin or fur, 3 to $3\frac{1}{2}$ material 60 in wide is required.

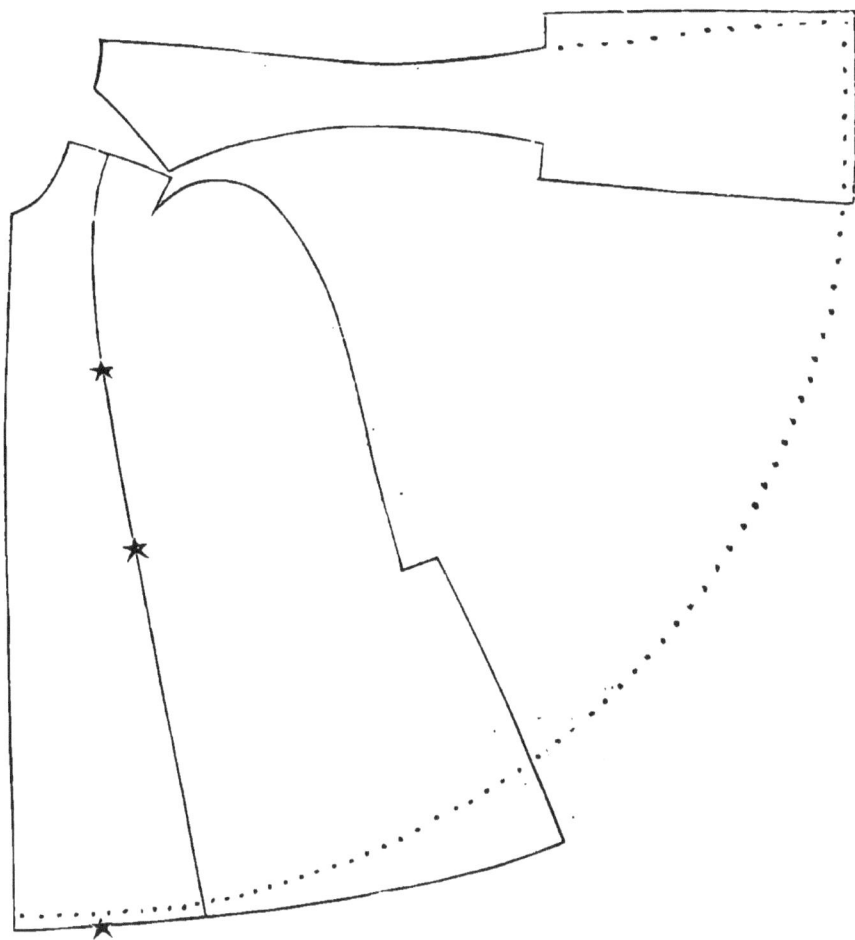

PATTERN FOR RUSSIAN AND PLAIN CIRCULAR.

RUSSIAN CIRCULAR.

The quantity of material required will be twice the length in double-width goods. Care should be taken to measure from the top of shoulder line. The other measures are taken the same as in dolman, omitting the third sleeve measure.

The front is drafted according to diagram, the upper front being lapped over the under front as far as the star at the lower part, and are then sewed together, excep tthe space between stars through which the arm passes.

The back is drafted as many inches below the waist line as desired, before allowing for plaits.

The front and back should both be cut lengthwise on the goods, the nap running down when made in cloth, and up when plush or velvet is used.

When finished, this circular should measure around the bottom from 2 to 2½ yards not counting the plaits.

PLAIN CIRCULAR.

The quantity of material required, is twice the length from top of shoulder line in double-width goods.

Draft according to outside lines of Russian circular, except below waist line in back where the dotted line should be used. Care must be taken to keep the length at side, the same as front and back.

In cutting the plain circular, lay the pattern so that the front and back lines are perpendicular to each other. Be careful to get both fronts on the selvedge, and the nap of the cloth to run the same way. This garment has but one seam only in the back and the shoulder seam as seen in cut.

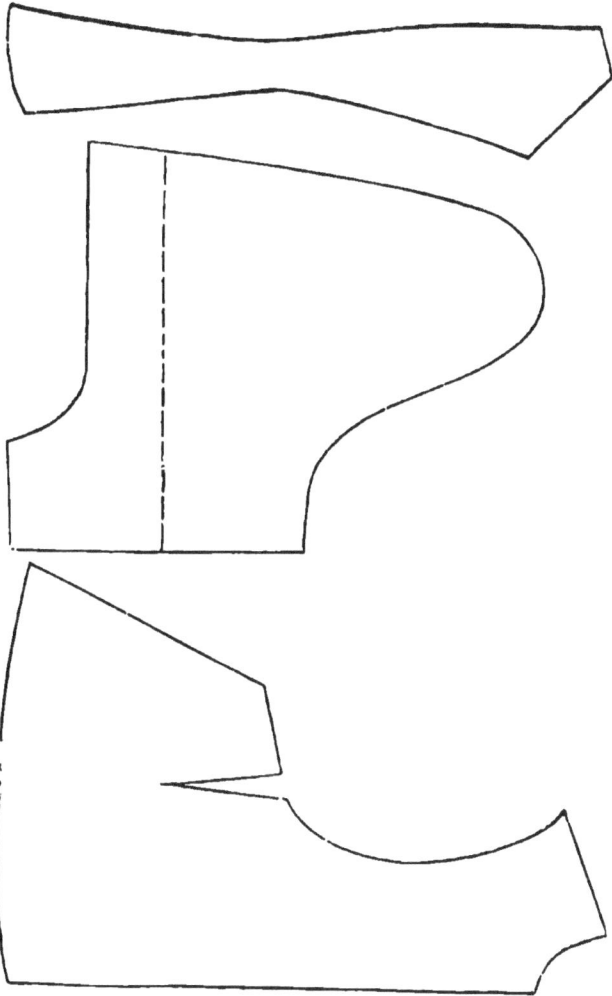

DOLMAN.

RIDING HABIT.

The waist of a riding habit is made the same as ordinary basque, except that it is quite short in front and over the hips. It is sometimes cut off entirely below the waist line and a postillion back is added. The basque also is sometimes made without a seam in the back, when this is done, an extra slope is of course taken off at the sides, in order to taper the waist to the proper size.

The skirt of a riding habit is cut long enough to lay on the floor several inches in the back and right side. The front and left side is sloped like a train skirt, about one-half yard longer. The skirt fits neatly over the front and hips. Allowance is generally made in a tailor-cut dress for the bend of the knee. Amateurs should not attempt to allow this fullness without great care in measuring.

It is usual for ladies to wear pants under a riding habit. These are made by tailors exactly like a gentleman's pants, fitting neatly to the figure, and may be worn with a strap under the boot, or the boots may be worn outside. They may be cut by the rules given in this book for boy's pants.

The best material for making a riding habit, for wearing in winter, is heavy stockinet or jersey cloth, as it wears better and is much warmer than lady's cloth, which is more suitable for spring and autumn.

The waist should be lined and padded thoroughly like a gentleman's coat.

The pants should be lined with chamois skin.

About five yards of double-width goods is sufficient for making a full habit, waist, skirt and pants.

The colors mostly used are dark blue and black; green and brown are sometimes used, but are more apt to fade.

W.H.MILLER SC

RIDING HABIT WAIST.

This cut shows how the inside of Habit Waist must be Padded to set nicely, inside of slender ladies' coat or waist may be finished in the same way with the exception of the whale bones, the latter should only be used for stout ladies if at all. Rules of Basque No. 5, makes a pretty front of a Riding Habit.

A nice way to put in whale bones is to cover the bones first with silk or a piece of the same lining as used in waist, and fasten along the seam about two inches apart, always stretch the seams tight against the bones.

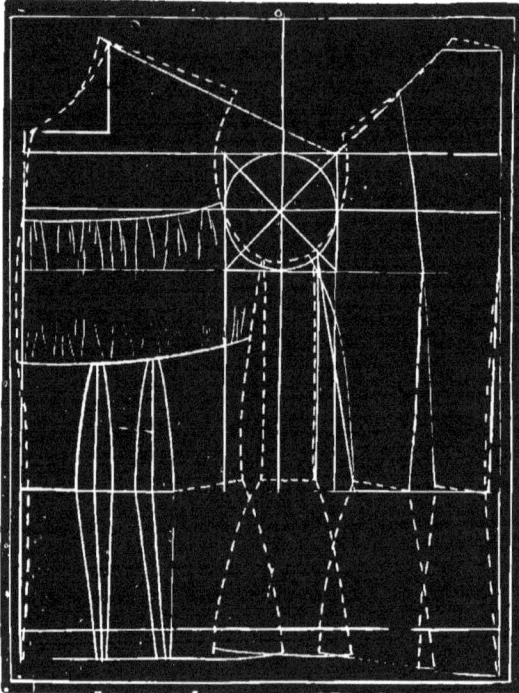

DIAGRAM OF REFORMED WAIST.

REFORM WAIST AND CORSET COVER.

Many ladies are recommended by their physicians to discard corsets entirely and wear instead a body with buttons attached, so that the weight of the clothing may be carried by the shoulders instead of the hips. This reform waist may be bought in the stores, but they are rather expensive; a knowledge of the A. L. T. S. will enable any one to make her own.

The diagram of plain basque, or the one with English back, will make either a corset cover or reform waist. For the latter one row of buttons should be placed one and one-fourth inches below waist line, and another row one and one-half inches below the first row.

The seam in the back may be carried up to the shoulder as in diagram if preferred. When this is done, the back should be made broader at waist line by increasing the distance between dots A and C. A basque may be cut in this way, and is becoming to those who wish to appear more slender. If desired, in making the corset cover, one dart may be used, and the seam may then be carried to the shoulder in front.

This waist is made according to fancy in the front or back, but is always cut on the same principle. The diagram represents one with a yoke. Below this, and over the bust only, a bias piece may be inserted. This should be faced down the front with a straight piece of material, and allowance should be made for fullness of about two inches less than double the width of front. The lower part is sloped down one-half inch deeper in the middle, then up two inches to under-arm gore seam   if correctly cut the grain of material will run straight at this seam. The body should be faced below the waist line and buttons placed as in the description for the plain reform waist.

The drawers and skirts worn with this waist should all be

made with yokes; button-holes should be placed at convenient distances, so that they correspond with the buttons on the waist to which they are to be fastened.

The neck should be cut somewhat lower than usual or the trimming will be visible. A long or short sleeve may be worn with this waist, or the trimming may form a sleeve.

Undervests and drawers can be bought woven in one piece, or if preferred, they may be sewed together. It is unnecessary to wear any other garment under this waist; the merino can of course be changed with the season.

Those ladies who prefer wearing corsets, may use the reform waist as a corset cover. The buttons may or may not be used.

The ease, comfort and beneficial effects from wearing a waist of this kind must be apparent to all.

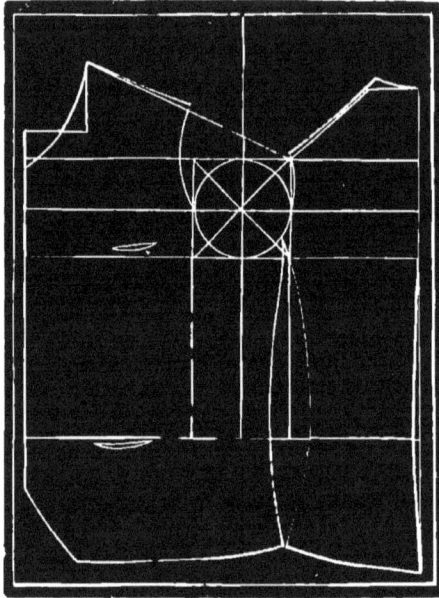

BOY'S JACKET.

MEASURES FOR BOYS SUIT.

Jacket.

1. Neck,   -   -   -   11½ Inches.
2. Arm's-eye, -   -   -   -   -   11   "
3. Bust, -   -   -   -   -   -   29   "
4. Waist,   -   -   -   -   -   - 25   "
5. Length of back, -   -   -   -   12¾   "
6. Length of front,   -   -   - 11¼   "
7. Under arm, -   -   -   -   -   7   "
8. Inside measure of sleeve, -   -   10   "
9. Wrist measure,   -   -   -   - 7   "

Rules for Drafting Jacket. .

Proceed as usual in drafting outside lines as in lady's plain basque. There are no darts required, as children's garments are loose-fitting: Allowance must be made for tucks and plaits, if desired.

Rules for Drafting Sleeves.

1. Line 1, inside measure, one-third of diameter of arm's-eye added, marking dot A, at inside measure, and B at end of line.

2. Line 2 is one-half of arm's-eye measure.

3. Line 3, parallel to line 1, make dot C on line 2 at one-half of arm's-eye measure.

4. Line 4, parallel to line 2, from line 1 to 3 from dot B.

5. Line 5, parallel to line 2 from dot A.

6. Line 6, parallel to line 2, one-third of diameter of arm's-eye, and mark dot D on line 3.

7. Dot E, on line 2, is one-half the distance from line 1 to dot C; then draw line 7 from dot E to line 5, parallel with line 1.

8. Dot F is in the centre of line 5.

9. Dot G is in the centre of line 3, between dot D and end of line 4.

10. Place the point of square on dot B, with long arm resting on dot F, and mark dot H at one-half the wrist measure.

11. Curve for the top of upper sleeve, from dot A to the junction of line 7 and 6, up to dot C, and down to dot D.

12. Curve for lower sleeve, from H to F, and up to D.

13. Curve for the inside of sleeve from B to A, one-half inch inside of line 1.

14. Curve for the outside of sleeve is from H to G.

15. This sleeve can be made tighter, and used for children's dresses.

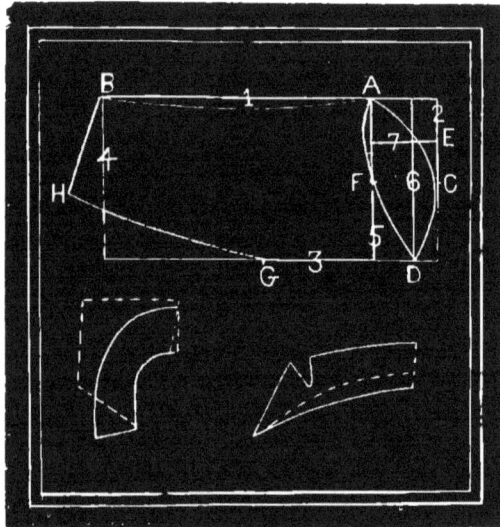

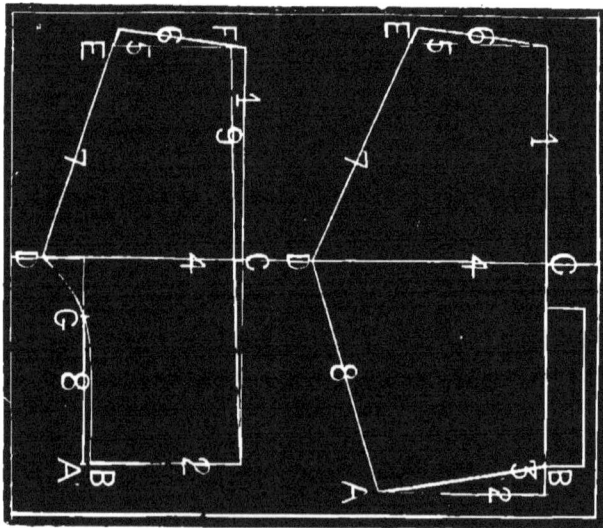

BOY'S PANTS.

Pants.

Outside measure	- - - -	15 Inches.
Inside "	- - - - -	7½ "
Waist,	- - - - -	23 "
Hip,	- - - - - -	32 "

RULES FOR DRAFTING.
(*Back of Pants.*)

1. Draw line 1, one inch longer than outside measure.

2. Line 2 is one-fourth of waist measure, add three-fourths of an inch and make dot A.

3. On line 1, one inch to the left of line 2, make dot B.

4. From dot B draw line 3 to dot A.

5. Make dot C on line 1 the height of inside measure.

6. Draw line 4 from dot C, parallel to line 2, to one-fourth of hip measure add three-fourths of an inch and make dot D.

7. Draw line 5 from the end of line 1, to one-half of knee measure add one-fourth of an inch, and make dot E.

8. Draw lines from A to D, from D to E, and extend it half an inch below dot E, and draw line 6.

9. Make a dart in centre of line 3 three-fourths of an inch wide.

(*Front of Pants.*)

1. Draw line 1, the length of outside measure.

2. Draw line 2, from end of line 1, one-fourth of waist measure, and make dot A.

3. One-fourth of an inch to the left of A make dot B.

4. Make dot C, on line 1, the height of inside measure, and draw line 4, one-fourth of hip measure, less three-fourths of an inch.

5. Draw line 5, from end of line 1, one-half of knee measure, less one-fourth of an inch, and make dot E.

6. Half an inch to the right of line 1, on line 5, make dot H, draw line from junction of lines 2 and 1 to dot H, for slope of side.

7. Draw a line from D to E, and extend it one-half inch, and draw line 6.

8. Two inches to the left of dot D draw a line to dot B, and curve for front of pants as shown in diagram.

9. In cutting out the pants be sure to follow the inside lines 3, 6 and 9.

10. Outside piece to the left of back, can be cut with the pants for a lap under at pocket, or it can be sewed on.

For Ladies' and Children's drawers use same measure and draft by the rule as boy's pants, width for gather may be added as much extra as would be desired according to taste ; if bloomers are desired follow the rule of bathing suit-pants.

To make the Boy's Jacket with pleats, allow twice as much for every pleat as you want to make the pleats wide, or, if no lining is used make the pleats first, then lay the pattern on and cut around.

In making Boy's Overcoat extend down to desired length. They are generally double-breasted, which is made by allowing more lap in the front.

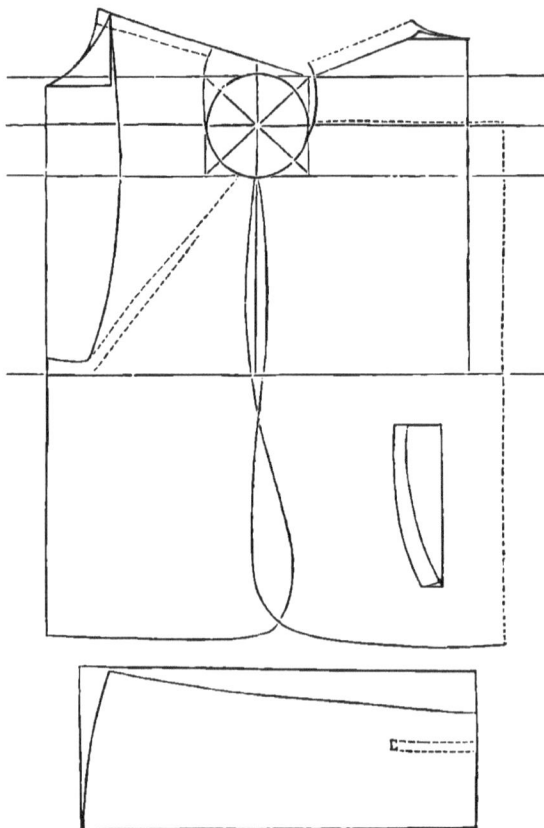

GENT'S SHIRT.

GENT'S SHIRT.—(Taking Measures).

1. For neck measure use the size of collar worn, or take a smooth measure around neck next to skin, low down, and add one inch to it.

2. Remove coat and take the arm's eye measure as for a lady's basque.

3. Take chest measure, measuring entirely around the form, over the vest. Take an easy measure.

4. Take under-arm measure same as for lady's basque, measuring down to the top of hip bone at side.

5. Take shoulder measure same as for lady's basque.

6. Take length of shirt measure from front of neck down in front to length desired.

7. Take length of bosom in same way.

8. Take arm to elbow and arm to wrist measures same as for a lady's basque.

Diagram shows plain how to draft a shirt, the outlines are the same as lady's basque, with the exception of the shoulder. Take off the front from one to two inches and add it to the back shoulder which is stitched on the front forming a yoke. Shoulder can be cut as short as desired.

See cut for shape of sleeve. Make top of sleeve from two to three inches wider than arm's eye measure if gathers desired. Sloped down to wrist and make allowance for gathers which are sewed to cuff or wrist-band. The seam may be sewed up and cut open on the top of wrist, which will prevent the annoyance of cuff buttons to a gentleman who does a great deal of writing. A two inch facing around top of sleeve is necessary, and a shirt that is faced from the neck to one inch below the arm-holes all around, is far more durable.

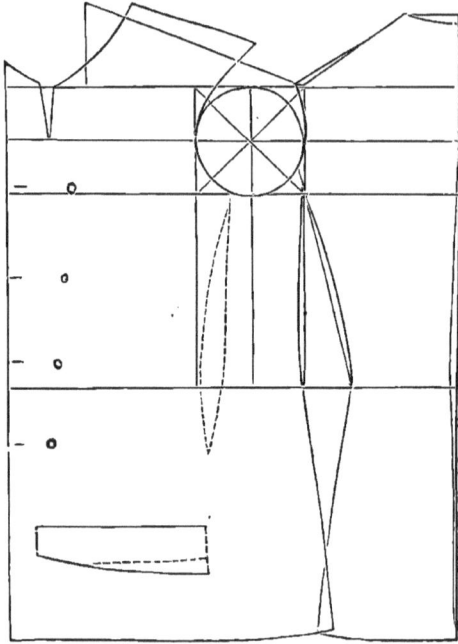

GENT'S COAT OR DRESSING GOWN.

GENTLEMEN'S COAT OR DRESSING GOWN MEASURES.

Remove coat and take arm's eye measure same as for lady's basque, loose not tight. Take chest **or bust** measure. Take waist measure smoothly, not tight. Take back, shoulder and under-arm measure same as lady's basque. All measurures are taken over the vest and under the coat.

RULES FOR DRAFTING.

Gentlemen's coat, smoking jacket or dressing gown of any kind may be measured or cut on the same principle with the exception of neck. Back of neck is sloped ½ inch below back line. On line 11, 2 inches from neck line make a mark and slope the front neck down. This throws the shoulder seam over the arm and away from the neck, and gives a square shoulder as a gentlemen's garment is cut different from a lady's. As many inches as you wish to turn over for collar or to make it double breasted add to the front, which is generally from 2½ to 3 inch. A small dart of about ½ inch deep and from 2 to 2½ inches long is required at the neck. This is done by cutting into the goods and sewing up again as you see in diagram. The latter rule may be adopted for a lady's double-breasted coat. For dressing gown or smoking jacket the dotted lines are not used. For dressing gown and wrapper extend down to length required. In drafting sleeve for gent's garment use lady's coat sleeve and add from 1½ to 2 inches to the average measure. Use less bent as a gentlemen's sleeve is nearly straight.

Gentlemen's garments should have as much as five or six layers of padding on top of shoulder tapering with less layers around arm-hole and lined with canvas. Padding must be catstitched on the canvas, latter should reach to the edge of the coat in the front. Garments for house use don't require so much pading. Smoking jackets are generally made of velvet plush, cashmere, and any color desired. Cuffs and collars can be made of fancy quilted silk or satin of different color, with cord and buttons to match.

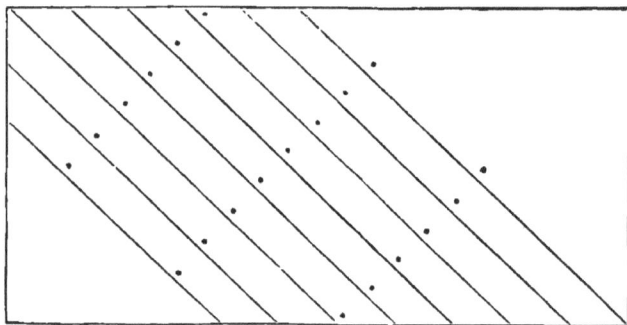

GUIDE FOR CUTTING BIAS.

Cut the end of material straight, so that it is exactly perpendicular to the selvedge, then fold it down to the selvedge and cut through the fold, laying aside the triangle for future use. Place the short end of square evenly on the bias side, and measure on long square the width desired, do this several times, as shown in guide. Rule lines through the dots thus made, and a true bias is obtained.

RULES FOR CUTTING.

All seams must be allowed except in neck and arm's-eye. One-half inch is enough, except under the arms, where the seams should be somewhat deeper. It is *absolutely necessary* to use a *tracing wheel,* in order to have your lines *perfectly true.*

After the dress is well cut, it must be made with great care, paying strict attention to the rules.

It is economy to use good material for lining.

Be careful always to lay the cloth so that both lining and outside run the same way, as your dress will be sure to wrinkle if either one or the other is on the bias.

In CUTTING VELVET, the *nap* must run up, in PLUSH likewise, in SEAL PLUSH *down.*

In cloth nap down inside of fold is the right side of cloth, in cutting plaid be sure to match stripes in waist, skirt and trimming which can always be done. Straight fronts and backs in waist lines should be cut the latter, which can easy be done in our system of cutting, if all rules are carefully observed, we guarantee perfection.

GENERAL REMARKS.

Changing seams in different ways from the general rules, for instance to give a slender lady a larger appearance, throw the front seam next to darts further back by taking off the under-arm gore and adding to the front. The darts above waist line may be drafted more slanting towards the back. Be careful in stiching darts to run them very tapering, a trifle higher than traced. The side-body next to back may be made more rounding, which some ladies prefer.

CUTTING FOR THE DEFORMED.

Very few forms are exactly alike on both sides. One shoulder may be shorter ; one hip higher ; one under-arm measure less; one side of neck larger, and so on. The only way to make a perfect fit for such forms is to measure *both sides,* and to make a drafting for each side. But where the differences are slight, it is best to aim to *hide the deformity* by drafting to the largest shoulder, shortest under-arm measure, and so on. In badly deformed cases take a piece of chalk and mark down the center of back, center of front, and also where you wish the different seams to come. Now measure each piece separately around bust and around waist, and make a separate drafting for each piece, using actual measures as taken for that piece. The worst hunch-back may be perfectly fitted in this way.

RULES FOR BASTING.

A basting thread must be *run* on the *line of the waist.*

Baste carefully, so that lining and outside are perfectly smooth.

In basting up the waist, commence at the waist line, and go up, then commence again at the waist line, and go down. The most troublesome seam in the whole waist, is the curved side body seam, which comes next to the back. In basting this seam, on one side of the back, commence at the waist line, and go up as in other seams, holding the outward curved seam toward you. The other side must be pinned at the waist line, and at intervals up the seam, then commence basting at the top, holding the outward curved seam toward you as in the other side.

Never run several stitches at a time in basting, but take a single stitch, one by one, about one-fourth of an inch apart. Use cotton suitable to material.

In sewing up seams. do not have the *machine* stitch too short, or it will draw.

Nick the seams, so that the waist will spring nicely into the figure, and then press them all open. If you wish to finish with Tailor-like neatness, turn in the edges and slip stitch them together, instead of whipping the seams as is the general custom.

No Hook and Eye pieces are required, but instead a *Waist-band* should be put inside the dress, to keep it in place.

If *Whalebones* are used, *casings* must be cut on the *bias* and sewed on loosely by *hand. Ribbon* may be used if preferred, but must also be sewed on almost as if ruffled. This to keep the bones in place very tight. They must each be fastened in several places along each seam.

The *Casings* must, as a rule, be run about two inches below the waist line, and about an even heighth with the dart all round. Under the arms they may be a little higher.

In our system whalebones are not necessary.

The above way of turning the cloth in finishing seams is not suitable in heavy material as it would show on the outside of waist after it is pressed. Neat overhanding preferable and would recommend it in all cases, where goods will not fray.

LININGS, PLAITINGS, RUFFLES, COLORS, Etc.

If the silesia, drilling or other material used for lining the waist is cut crosswise it is less apt to stretch. It is economy to use a good quality of material for lining, as a poor lining will wear out sooner than the outside goods, and the result will be that the seams will stretch, and the waist lose its shape.

A dress should not be made so tight as to draw. The corset should be pulled in as required, and the waist should be fitted over it easily and without wrinkles. The seams will stretch and fray out, if this rule is not followed. The same corset should be worn with the dress that it was measured and fitted over, as different corsets change the figure. A dréssmaker should make it a rule never to measure a lady over old or ill-fitting corsets.

Velvet, plush, hernani and other thin goods should be lined with silk. It should be used with the heavy goods because it makes a neater fit, and with the thin goods because they are transparent, and it will have a more pleasing effect.

A good silk dress should also be lined with silk to match the dress in color. Surah or some inexpensive silk may be used. By following this rule, when the dress begins to wear out or the seams to draw, the lining is not visible, as it surely would be under other circumstances.

In making a close *kilt plaiting* for trimming, allow two and one-half to three yards for every yard required. A close *box-plaiting* requires the same quantity. Allowance should be made for a kilt skirt on the same principle. It is well to use a nicked card to measure each plait, and keep them uniform.

For a gathered ruffle, allow one-fourth to one-half yard extra for every yard.

Diagram of the Pattern in One or More Sizes and One or More Designs.

PATENT APPLIED FOR.

DIRECTIONS FOR CUTTING.

These patterns are in three sizes, 36, 38, 40, Bust, marked thus:

40 Bust, straight line, thus ————————

38 " short lines, thus — — — —

36 " dotted lines, thus ....

The extra Bust Curve, on Pattern, is for large ladies only.

The lines extending from Waist line are for box Plaits, Back like Cut.

The lines not extended are for plain Jersey Basques.

All seams must be allowed except neck and arms eye, for the above sizes, stitching must go in the lines.

Increase or decrease of these sizes can be made by stitching inside or outside of the above sizes.

Full directions how to use the Patterns (on opposite page) in different ways under the heading "How to be Your Own Dress Maker."

These Patterns are manufactured on Paper and Linings.

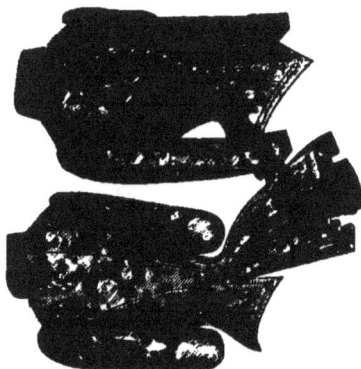

Copyright, 1884, by Mrs. E. Gartland.

Cut shows two designs, Pointed Bodice and Box Pleat Back.

Be Your Own Dress Maker

FULL SIZE

GLOVE-FITTING

Paper ✢ Pattern

Given with Each Book.

Easy Practical Lessons in Cutting, Fitting and Making Dresses at Home

---

INTRODUCTION.

The cost of having dresses, of simple and inexpensive material, really well made frequently exceeds the price of the material itself, hence the desirability of a lady understanding how to make a dress for herself, supposing she has time at her disposal for work of the kind. Knowing how to cut and fit is not knowing how to make a dress. Our purpose is to go through all the details in as practical a manner as possible to help those of our readers who may be desirous of learning, or whose position demands that they make a good appearance, yet whose means may be somewhat inadequate to pay what really clever dressmakers are obliged to charge for the amount of time which a well-made dress takes to complete.

We desire particularly to indicate that dressmakers generally do not charge too highly for good cut and fit combined with the great amount of work which modern fashion decrees a dress requires ; and further, we may remark, that the large quantity of material which pleatings, kiltings, and draperies necessitate is calculated to astonish those who really do not understand how a dress is made.

Many of our correspondents ask this question:—"How am I to make my allowance of so and so sufficient to supply me with the needful dresses for such and such occasions.

Our reply to such a question is, make some of your dresses yourself. It is quite astonishing how some young ladies, who are possessed of good to taste and industry, can dress well upon a small allowance, while others spend much money with a very inadequate result in the way of an appearance.

If a lady makes a dress for herself she will probably be enabled to purchase material of a better quality, which will wear longer, and keep in much better condition than commoner material.

As we know not what the future has in store for us, it is well to prepare for emergencies, and one of the most useful is to know how to keep up a good appearance at a small cost.

Ladies who know enough about dressmaking to be enabled to direct a maid, or other seamstress, to work for them or their families, will also find the practical knowledge useful.

When a new dress is required, one of the first things to consider is the style in which it should be made; this, in most instances, can be easily determined by referring to the numerous fashion illustrations in our Journal and Supplements.

Next calculate the quantity of material it will take—this we shall endeavor to assist our readers in doing.

Purchase all the materials you require before beginning your work; you will thus affect a great saving of time.

If you are complete novice in dress making, we think if you will study the directions, in the order that we give them, you will succeed.

If you desire to attempt a difficult dress, you will find a great help in purchasing a trimmed pattern of the dress to work from, or a pattern of any difficult part of the dress.

In order to give ladies an opportunity of estimating for themselves what materials should be purchased for a dress, we will take as an example the illustration shown in this book, page   , to fit a medium figure, which we take at, height 5 feet 4 inches; bust, 36 inches; waist, 23 inches.

Materials required for dress shown in illustration:

19 yards plain fabric 24 inches wide. If of striped or figured material, 20 yards. Omit tucks 2 yards less will make a dress with the same effect.

Half-yard sarsnet, for lining basque, sleeves, and collar.

2 dozen buttons.

2 yards lining for sleeves, bodice, 1 yard wide, and pocket ; the lining should be firm but soft.

4½ yards alpaca for skirt foundation.   Cambric muslin or silk may be used.

2 yards Caledonian, for lining foot of skirt.

3 yards braid, for binding bottom of skirt.

Steels or whalebones for bodice ; one 6 inches in length, four 8 inches, four 9 inches, one 11 inches.

Steels for skirt ; one 22 inches, and one 27 inches.

1½ yards crinoline.

6 yards binding or galloon for bone casings.

1½ oz. curled horsehair for small mattress, or dress improver.

Three reels of cotton, color of dress.

One ¼-oz. reel of silk or twist.

1¾ yards webbing for tight size and skirt band.

One packet hooks and eyes, fives.

Three-quarter yard cotton elastic, about ½ inch wide.

One piece of tape 1½ inch wide.

4 yards ribbon velvet, 1½ inch wide.

TOOLS AND ARTICLES REQUIRED FOR DRESS-MAKING

One paper short white pins.

One packet needles, No. 7 Sharps.

One packet straw needles. No. 6.

An inch tape measure.

One pair large sharp scissors.

One pair buttonhole ditto.

A lead cushion.

A wooden roller, or cheap rolling pin covered with flannel, fastened on it with quite a flat herringbone seam.

An ironing blanket.

A tracing wheel and piercer.

Tailor's square or yard stick with inches and parts of inch.

Metal belt.

Instruction book.

One flat iron.

Lap board.

DIRECTIONS FOR MEASUREMENT.

It is quite unnecessary to give directions for taking a pattern, as it needs a great deal of experience to take one properly. Ladies who desire to make their own dresses, and who find the bodice pattern given with our book, so very different to their own size that they cannot conveniently alter it, can always have a bodice and sleeve pattern cut to their measure, either flat or made up, sent direct from our Office. When once you have a good fitting pattern, take care of it, as it will serve for years, with trifling alterations.

Always measure with a marked inch tape.

We note this, as some persons use cord for measuring—a great mistake as cord is so very elastic.

Take all measures over a dress. Measure around the waist tightly ; round the throat; round the bust loosely—just under the arms and over the fullest part of the bust. In front, from the hollow of the throat to the waist. From the prominent neck-bone at the back to the bend of the waist. From under the arm to the waist. Across the back from point to point of join of side-piece next back. For the shoulders, from the side of throat to top of arm.

For sleeve, round the top of the arms, putting the tape about an inch below arm-pit. Length of back of arm, bending the elbow measuring from the top of side-piece next back to the wrist-bone Measure the front of arm, about $1\frac{1}{2}$ inch from front side-piece seam to the wrist. Another important measure, now the sleeves are so much arched at the top, is to put the tape from the bone of the elbow to the shoulder-bone, which gives the measure for the proper curve a the top of sleeve. Full directions in measuring according to rules of system for any garment.

MEASURE OF THE BODICE PATTERN,

Which we give in these the size. It is without turning.

The waist measures 22 to 28 inches.

Throat, $13\frac{1}{2}$ to 16 inches.

Bust, 36, 38, 40. Extra Bust curve 44.

From throat to waist-front, 14 to 16 inches.

From neck-bone at back to waist, 15 to 16 inches.

Across back, 12, 14, 15, inches

Under arm to waist, 7, 8, 9 inches.

Shoulder, 4½ to 6½ inches.
Around the arm over the shoulder, 14 to 16 inches.
Sleeve measure: inside 19 to 16 inches.
Size around top of arm, 14½ to 16 inches,
Slope from shoulder to elbow, 14½ inches.

To take a pattern easily from our diagram, put some tissue paper over the diagram and lightly run over each separate part with a tracing-wheel; or, if you have not a tracing-wheel, mark the tissue with a soft lead pencil; a hard lead pencil must not be used, or you will cut through and destroy the Pattern.

TO ALTER A PATTERN.

If on measuring you find the bodice pattern we have given too large for you, pin each part together, one edge just passing over the other flatly, measure round the decreased pattern according to the directions for measurement already given, and if you find it still too large continue to take it in a little more at every seam except those of the bust pleats. Cut off half the overlapping portion of each edge. If the pattern is too full in the bust it will improve the figure to fill up with small pads of wadding made in a circular form about 4 inches across.

If the pattern is too small piece it on a piece of paper and pin closely at the edges; cut it with a margin of the paper you pinned all around; treat all four parts of the bodice pattern in the same manner, allowing equal additions to each; do not add to the piece between the two bust pleats; if more fullness is required for the bust, cut a small piece away from each part of bodice that joins to the strip between the bust pleats.

TO CUT BODICE LINING.

Place the front of the pattern upon the lining (double, as purchased) about 2 inches from the selvage at the centre of the bodice, that is, half way between the neck and waist; pin closely all round, making quite sure that the lining is perfectly smooth. Then pin on the side-piece next front, in the space left level with the front; the highest point this side-piece should lie straight with a weft thread of the lining. Next place the back pattern on the lining beneath the

front, and pin first 1½ inch from the selvage at the top of the neck,
smooth it with your hand straight down from neck to waist, pin
firmly and closely all round.

Now you come to an important part in cutting, that is, the side-piece
next back. The point must be carefully placed quite straight with a
weft thread of the lining 1½inch from selvage. The part marked *
must lie ¾ inch from the selvage, straight with a weft thread. By
observing this the side which joins the back will curve in the proper
direction to fit with back, and will be nearly on the cross; failing to observe this, you will never make the back of a dress look well.

The back of the sleeve, must be quite on the straight of the lining.
Place your sleeve pattern in the space of lining left by the back. Now
you have fixed all the patterns upon the lining, you proceed to cut,
leaving ¾ inch turning all parts but the front and bust pleats; these
remain uncut until the material is tacked to the lining. Now, with
a small awl, or piercer, pierce all round the pattern at intervals of ¾
inch; be sure to pierce carefully at every point of a pattern most
particular at waist lines which is marked in our pattern with dots
. . . . as the pieces go together. You will understand further
on why this is an important rule to observe.

Now take your pattern off the lining, being careful to put it all together, and tie it up and mark it; you should never pin your pattern
in putting it away, as it is apt to tear it, and a really good pattern
once taken is valuable.

TO CUT BODICE IN MATERIAL.

For silk, woollen, or cotton, the material should always be double,
so that you cut the corresponding parts together. The lining has now
to be pinned closely upon the material in the same way as has been
described for the pattern upon the lining, except that you do not leave
any material beyond the edge of the lining If you are using a figured material with an up-and-down pattern, take care that the pattern
is right before cutting, or you may waste a good deal of it. If striped,
be most careful in cutting so the stripes meet where the seams join in
the centre of the back, and at the side-piece next back. Now, when
all the separate parts of the of the bodice and sleeves are pinned upon
the material cut; unpin the fronts and place the material upon the

lining, back to back ; pin the material to the lining at the shoulder
and neck, material towards you, and smooth with the hand from the
shoulder downwards, pinning as you smooth, so as to slightly stretch
the material upon the lining. After having thus stretched it downwards, stretch and pin it across in the same manner, smoothing it with
the hand. After having pinned each piece of the bodice in the manner
described, commence the tacking. You must now have the lining
towards you. Tack with white or any odd lengths of colored cotton
that will show upon the material. In tacking observe the piercing at
the corners of the pattern (to which we have before called attention).
Put the needle into the piercings of these corners; be most careful to
do this at every point. In tacking the material upon the lining tack
with stitches about the same length as the piercings, but you need not
be particular about working through the piercings, except at the
points. The sleeves must be treated in the same way as described for
the bodice.

TO PUT THE BODICE TOGETHER.

1st.—Begin by taking up the bust pleats; start at front pleat at the
top and pin so as to make the tacking threads exactly correspond ; the
second pleat must be taken up in the same manner. When pinned,
tack closely and firmly so that they cannot slip or move in the stitching. Now lay the two fronts aside for the present.

2nd.—Take up the two back-pieces, pin them together, observing to
put the pin exactly through the two corresponding pierced holes by
holding them up and passing the pin first through the pierced hole of
one piece of the back and then the other, and then putting the pin
through about half an inch lower down as usual. You will, of
course, pin from the neck downwards, carefully matching the tacking,
and after pinning tack closely.

3rd.—Take up the side-pieces next the back, and this is one of the
parts needing the utmost care and attention if you would have your
dress look like the work of a practical dressmaker. Place the pin
through the points of the side-piece and back (see the points marked
* and * in diagram). Do not forget the need of observing the marked
points. The rounded part of the side-piece must be slightly stretched
in pinning it to back, holding the back just easily. Observe, the

rounded part of the side-piece next back should be shorter than the corresponding part of the back ; the object of this is to make the back set perfectly. Be very careful that the little fullness is equally divided, so that when tacked and stitched it is imperceptible. The corresponding side-piece must now be treated in the same way.   .

4th.—Next pin and tack the side-pieces next front, and if you have not previously used the pattern to make perfectly sure of its fitting, let the turnings of the two seams be outside instead of in their places, as this will materially assist you in enlarging or taking in, as the case may be. Our experience is that it is so much better in fitting to have your material on the right side, that is outside, as it will be worn, because it allows for the size taken up by the seams when next you. After you have pinned closely these side-pieces to the fronts and to the side-pieces previously joined to the back, leave the pin in, and do not tack either of these four seams because the pins will be easier to remove and to make any alteration required.

5th.—The shoulders are the next parts requiring your attention ; these are also pinned with the seams outside ; stretch the front shoulder in pinning it to the back, not omitting to observe the pierced holes at the points ; slightly notch all.the seams at the waist to allow for the curve of the figure. Now your bodice is ready for fitting.

6th.—Observe the same rule in pinning and tacking sleeves as have been given for the bodice, first pinning and tacking the front seam, beginning at the top of sleeve. Now begin the back seam at the top, pin straight till you reach the elbow, leave the fullness where it seems to fall naturally, and continue to pin below it to the waist. Now return to the fullness at the elbow, which you must gather and pin flatly in its place, and tack the seam dowh ; notch the seam of the front of sleeve, turn the sleeve right side outwards, and it is ready for fitting.

FITTING.

It is quite possible that, however well your pattern may be cut, and however carefully you may have tacked it, the difference in the elasticity of the material may slightly effect the fit, and some alteration may be needed. Notch the turnings at the waist three times at intervals of about one inch, excepting those which are outside ; cut open the bust-pleats to within an inch of the tops, and notch in the same manner. Put your bodice on gently, so that you remove no pins and break no tackings. Have a large supply of good pins at hand.

Begin your fitting from the throat by pinning the front of the bodice, observing to put the first pin through the pierced holes at points. Pin to the tacking threads down the front of bodice, making no alteration at present, unless the bodice is to tight, when of course you let it out so as to meet comfortably down the front. Pass the hand from the front towards the side-piece under the arm, and smooth the bodice so as to see if it fits sufficiently close to the figure; do not make it extremely tight, as the stitched seams will not give out to the same extent as the tacked ones. Care should be taken to let out both the seams of the side you are fitting to the same extent. If the bodice appears to be very tight, let out a little from the front, as, if too much increase is made at the side-piece seams, the arm-hole will be too large. Now pass the hand from the bust to the shoulder upwards and remove the pins if there is need of alteration.

Look well to the bust-pleats, and alter, should they be too high or too low. Sometimes there is need to take in a little at the middle seam of the back. Place a pin exactly at the bend of the waist, back and front—that is, if the tacking-thread is not already at the right place. See that the tacking-thread at the throat is in the right place; if too high or to low, mark the line it should be with a few pins, and notch within a quarter-inch of the fitting line.

Take the sleeve and slip it over the arm, put the elbow fullness to the elbow, and look to see if it is in the right position; carry your eye along the back seam of sleeve to the shoulder, and see that it is long enough, if not, pull it up to the requisite height, so that you can pin it to the armhole; if the elbow fulling is too high bend the arm and put a pin to mark the point of the elbow. Now we come to the front seam of sleeve. Turn under to the tacking-thread, put a pin into the sleeve through the tacking-line, and then pass it through the tacking at the armhole of the bodice. The front seam of sleeve should be about one and a half inch to the front of front side-piece seam. Go on turning down to the tacking-thread, and pinning the sleeve to the bodice till within two inches from the shoulder seam. Now look to the back of the sleeve, and see that the under part from the front seam to the back fits properly. Pin it so that it fits. What little fullness remains must be equally distributed at the top of the shoulder. See to the length of sleeve, and turn up to that required, pinning it to the proper length. Now remove the bodice by taking out the pins from the shoulder and side-piece next front of the unfitted side of bodice. By this method the pins are left in down the front, and if any alteration has been made you can tack a line down to the pins before removing them.

TO CORRECT THE FIT.

In some cases you may find that your bodice fits perfectly, when the following observations will not be needed; but lest the condition has not arrived, we will give you directions to follow closely to correct any misfitting part. This is done by tacking to the line of pins before removing them. Be sure, before removing the pins from the sleeve and armhole, tack closely round both sleeve and armhole, and run a few stitches down to mark the exact position of the front seam of the sleeve to the armhole. After having tacked exactly in accordance with these directions, remove all pins. You will have fitted one side only of the bodice, which should be the right-hand side. Now correct the left-hand side, pin all the original tackings of the two sides to correspond exactly with each other round the armhole, the neck, and at the under arm seams. If the bust-pleats have been altered, pin the seams very carefully together, and pin round the corrected tacking; turn the left-hand front towards you and tack to the pins.

TO MAKE BODICE.

Pin the front side-piece in position to side-piece next back, ready for tacking first and stitching afterwards.

Begin by stitching the front pleats, and be very careful to do this with precision, observing carefully the tackings. The fronts are for the present to remain detached from the side-pieces and shoulders until the back and side-piece seams are stitched, the buttonholes made, and the buttons sewn on.

Next take the buttonhole front, that is the right-hand front; take the bottom part of the bodice towards the right-hand. Turn the front down a quarter of an inch outside the original front tacking-thread, and with a needle and thread tack as you turn. Now, according to the material of the dress, take a piece of sarsnet ribbon, tape, or silk for facing; turn the inside of front of bodice towards you, and hem your facings just a shade nearer the edge of front than the tacking-thread; be most careful not to take a stitch through the right side. When you come to a bend of the waist you must full the facing slightly to give the proper spring when this is hemmed down to the bottom of the bodice. If the material of the bodice is thick, you must turn up the facing and cut away tne material and lining to within an eighth of an inch of the facing hem. If a thin material, cut only the lining in the same way. Now cut the material so that when the facing is hemmed down the second time it covers the edge, and makes the front neat inside. With the second hem of the facing, as with the first, be careful that your stitches are not taken through.

Now turn the outside of bodice uppermost, throat towards the right hand. Take an inch tape, and according to the size of the buttons measure for the hole; the small fashionable button used at present will take a half-inch bottonhole.

A button the size of a three-cent piece will take a five-eighths of an inch buttonhole, and one the size of a 10 ct. piece must have a three-quarter-inch buttonhole, and so on in proportion. To ensure the buttonholes being correctly cut to one size you must place a pin in the inch tape to the required measure, lay a pin on to the front edge tacking-thread, and tack a line down to the end of the measure, putting in a stitch, each time you shift the measure, till you get to the bottom of bodice.

It is always well to have proper tools for your work, therefore you will find that a pair of buttonhole scissors will cut much better buttonholes than an ordinary pair of scissors. When you have cut a buttonhole to the measure, turn the bodice round, with the front edge opposite you, and cut a tiny triangular piece out of the top of the buttonhole by making two slanting cuts of about an eighth of an inch, and then a straight cut crosswise. For small buttons the buttonholes should be about three-quarters of an inch apart. In this you must of course be ruled by the size of the button.

Now, to work a buttonhole properly, take the front edge of bodice towards you, have a needleful of the twist with which you intend working the buttonholes. Begin at the left side close end of buttonhole (not the end from which the triangle is cut), and sew over all round, taking care not to stretch the edge of the buttonhole; now bar the buttonhole all round by taking a stitch from the narrow end to the broad end, put your needle back above the opening of the triangle, and work a bar above it just the width of the cut; work to the close end of the other side, and repeat, so that you have a double bar of twist to work over, which raises and strengthens the buttonhole. Begin to work the buttonhole from the same end as you began to oversew it, let your left thumb-nail rest just below the bar of twist, and work closely and evenly all round.

The buttonholes finished, take the button side of front, with the same kind of facing as was used for buttonhole side. Take the neck of front to the right hand, the outer side towards you, hemming the facing one and a half inch from the tacking line, hem to the waist, where full in the same way as you did the facing of the first side; then continue plain to the bottom of the bodice.

Now turn the inside of front to you, and cut off the surplus part of front to within a quarter of an inch of the stitches of facing; turn the right side of bodice towards you and turn down the edge of front, so that the facing is just edge to edge with the material. Now tack the facing down through from the outside just at the tack of the button line; when you have tacked to the button line, hem the facing from bottom to top of bodice; take care that no stitch appears through.

To mark for buttons, take the two fronts, neck towards left hand, put a pin through the top stitch of buttonhole side of tacking thread; where the tacking for throat begins put the pin through to the corresponding tacking of button side of front; pin firmly together. Now get some one to hold the bodice just where you have pinned it, or pin it to a lead cushion; put a pin into the centre of the triangle at the top of buttonhole and through to the tacking line for the botton exactly opposite it.   Continue to place the pins through all the buttonholes for the entire length of the bodice, holding the buttonhole side rather tightly.

Buttons without shanks must be sewn on loosely; the cotton should be left about an eighth of an inch as a substitute for a shank, and after sewing the buttons strongly twist the cotton several times round the threads that form the substitute for the shank; this done, pin the frouts to the side-pieces, stretching the fronts to the side-pieces.

Next measure the waist from the inside of the bodice, holding the tape tightly immediately above the tacking line of the waist, with the end of the tape exactly to the edge of the waist buttonhole and to the corresponding button, holding the bottom of the bodice towards you. If the size of the waist needs alteration, enlarge or decrease equally from side-piece and front; begin by pinning from the waist line upwards gradually and carefully, so that the line remains quite even ; after this, pin from the waist line to the bottom of the bodice, tack it carefully. Now pin the shoulders, beginning at the pierced points of the neck on each side stretching the fronts of the shoulders in putting in each pin, so that the pierced points at the armhole end of shoulder meet. When closely tacked stitch the seams ; remove all tacking-threads from the bodice except those round the throat and armhole. Now cut the edges of all the turnings or seams very narrow and even, say ¼ of an inch is sufficient, next cut them in notches, this is to make them look neat, and lie flat, and to prevent the bodice from creasing when put on ; over-sew all the turnings, material side towards you, this makes the work neater. If the material is of a very frail description you must bind with narrow sarsnet ribbon instead of over-sewing. It will now be needful to open the seams ; lay them quite flat, and press them on a board covered with an ironing-blanket. If the bodice is of silk or velvet a second person must assist in holding it while the other passes the iron over it; the person holding the bodice should have the top of the seam in the hand. To press the bust pleats the person assisting should hold the seam under the arm and the front of bodice in a line with the top of the bust pleats. If you use whalebones you must next run on the casings, which should be of galloon or stay-binding. The casings should be under the buttons to the same height as front bust pleat, on all the bust pleats, and all other seams except the curve seams of side-piece next back. The back casing should be about six inches long—five inches above the waist and one or two below it.

Turn down a loop of the casing about three-quarters of an inch in length. Begin by sewing at the bottom of the loop so as to make it strong, run on the casing, easing it with the thumb so as to make it sufficiently loose for the bend of the bone. If you use the new bodice-steels you will not need casings as these steels are already covered ; they are sewn through the hole at the top and at distances of about two inches, stretching the seam after each sewing. Steels would not, however, need your attention until after you have turned up the bottom of bodice, but, unlike bones, they must be secured before sewing on the facing at bottom of the bodice.

Turn up the bottom of the bodice, beginning at the button side, fixing it with pins. As you turn it, see that you have it turned to a nice shape; when satisfactory, tack it up if you intend to have it simply faced. If you desire to have it corded, run a tacking-line to where the edge turns, remove the pins. To make the second side exactly like the first put a pin through the point of the first pleat and through the top of corresponding pleat of the other front; repeat this with the second pleats. Put a pin through the waist buttonhole to the waist button, then pin to the top of side-piece next front at the point, passing through the corresponding point of the other side-piece; you have your bodice right side out, pin closely the two tacking-lines round the under part of armhole from the point already indicated to the second seam of side-piece next back. This done, see that the two sides of bodice are quite flat at the seams, and along the line of the side turned up and tacked, put pins through to the second side, and before removing the pins run a line of tacking on the second side in the same place as the pins, after which remove the pins on the first side and you will have the bottom of the bodice perfectly even, when turn and tack it up; cut off all surplus material and face.

Should you prefer a corded waist, after having made the cording, for which we will give directions further on, you must lay your cording upon the tacking line and stitch as close to the cord as possible from the under side of it. When the cording is firmly stitched on, the bodice is made neat by hemming up the facing left on the cord, with great care that not a stitch goes through to the right side. Now, if you use bones you must cut them to the length of the casings, scrape them until they are quite thin at both ends; if this is not done they will soon wear through the bodice. Now put the bones in their casings through the loops left at the top, then run the loop so as to secure the bones in their places at the top, push the bones close to the bottom of the bodice and sew through the bones to the casing and turning of the bodice about an inch from the bottom of the bodice. Now take the top of the turning and bone casing together and push the bone down as tightly as you can hold it in place and sew it strongly at the top just below the loop. Sew a webbing band a quarter of an inch smaller than the size of waist of bodice to the bone casing and turning of the back seam immediately above the waist-line; fasten at the ends with two small hooks and eyes. This is called the size; it pulls and keeps the bodice in place at the back.

For the collar, measure the neck of bodice, place the pattern on a double piece of stiff muslin on the cross, pierce round the pattern and cut the muslin, allow half-inch turnings all round, cut the collar and facing also on the cross; pin the four thicknesses together, the wrong side of the material next the muslin, then the facing upon the mater-ial; pin smoothly and tack altogether through the pierced holes along the sides and across the toy. Next take the muslin and material at the bottom of the collar and tack it together, leaving the sarsnet free. This tacking is to mark the depth of collar as to where it should be stitched to the bodice. Stitch the ends and top, remove the tacking except at the bottom, turn the collar right side out and tack round about a quarter of an inch from the edge to hold the facing in its place. Put the lower tacking line of collar to the tacking line of neck of bodice; the collar is held towards you, and great care must be taken not to stretch the neck of the bodice; stitch through the ma-terial, leaving the facing free to be hemmed down on the inside. Put two small hooks and two loops on the collar, the hooks on the button-hole side about the same distance in as the buttonholes. The loops are placed in a line with the buttons. Take a piece of ribbon or binding about half an inch wide, tack it round the armhole inside the bodice, beginning at the seam of side-piece next front; tack it about an eighth of an inch from the lower edge, continue all round the armhole; be sure not to stretch the armhole nor full it; this must be tacked exactly to the armhole tacking, cut off, and turn down the end of the ribbon or binding.

TO MAKE THE SLEEVE.

Stitch exactly to your tacking, being quite sure that you have the fullness at the elbow in its right place; stitch the seams, open them, and over-sew if the sleeve is of woollen material; pass a roller covered with flannel down it, and press the seams flat; of course the sleeve must be inside out. Now turn up the bottom of sleeve to the required length and face with sarsnet or a piece of silk. Take care that not a stitch of the hem of facing goes through to the right side of sleeve. Turn the sleeve right side out and put on the trimming, supposing it is considered necessary. Next put in the sleeve; take the front seam of sleeve and put it exactly to the tacking which marks its position; have the inside of sleeve and bodice towards you, pin the sleeve and bodice tacking lines exactly to each other until within two inches of the shoulder seam; now go back to the under-seam from which you started and pin in the second side. When you come towards the top distribute the fullness equally along about three inches at the top. After pinning in tack closely; stitch the sleeve in strongly, cut the turnings off within about half an inch of the stitching, and over-sew the edge of armhole, sleeve, and binding together neatly.

SKIRT OF DRESS—LIKE ILLUSTRATION, No. 1.
IN THIS BOOK.

Foundations of skirts vary very little in shape. From the illustration we have given it will be quite easy to make the needful alterations for other styles ot dresses.

Begin by cutting the foundation of skirt—for this alpaca is frequently used—it measures 26 inches in width. For a skirt proportionate with the the the bodice pattern given: length of back, allowing for a medium-size crinolette, 43 inches; cut foundation 45½ inches, to allow for 2 inch hem and half-inch turning at waist. Skirt 2 to 2½ yards wider. Length of front 40 inches; cut 42½ (for hem and turning); width of bottom of skirt 2½ yards. The breadth next the front is cut into two gores, the straight sides of thess gores join the front breadth; the length for cutting this breadth is 43½ inches. Fold this breadth straight down the middle, and fold over at the double part ot breadth, that is the middle of breadth, 5 inches at the top, smoothing it with your hand so that it graduates off and slopes to within a quarter of yard of bottom of skirt; cut off the slope and cut down the remaining quarter of yard.

Now take the slope that you have cut off the gored sides, cut it down the middle, and join the straight sides to the gores.

Next spread the front gores of the skirt on a table, wrong side up; take the stiff lining that is to go round the foot, cut it about 12 inches in depth, this must be taken across the lining, not selvage-wise; cut enough to go along the joined breadths, edge to edge at the bottom, where tack it and fix it at the top, turning in about half an inch; tack it again, shaping it to the gores by turning it in at the joins. Now take the back breadth and line it in the same way, and hem along the top and down the joins. Face the whole with about 5 inches of the material of the dress, turn down and hemmed on the right side of the foundation, leaving edge of material to edge of foundation at the bottom. Now join back breadths to sides · this done, turn up the hem at the bottom.

First pin the breadths together at the seams at the top of the skirt (that is, the waist), folding the front breadths down the middle.

Take an inch tape, and put the end of it half an inch below the top edge of skirt; pin it firmly through the inch tape and material to a lead cushion or let some one hold it for you. Take the foot of the skirt in your left hand, hold the inch tape in your right hand tightly, being quite sure that you have both sides of your skirt flat and even. Put the pin through at the exact length you require the front of your skirt to be when finished; leave the pin through both breadths. Next measure the back breadth folded, as described for the front; measure the back as you have done the front, leaving it the exact length required for the dress when finished. Take the middle of backb readth of skirt and turn up from the pin at the back to the pin in front, graduating it to the front pin; this makes the sides the proper length. Pin the bottom edge quite through the facing, foundation, and lining; turn skirt inside out and hem up, taking care that the stitiches do not go through to the facing on the right side. Now put on the braid. Next, over-sew the seams, and press with a hot iron on the wrong side.

Take a piece of webbing and cut it five inches longer than the waist is to be when finished. Take a strip of the material of the dress, the length of the webbing and half inch wider, run it closely along one edge of the webbing, material towards you, leaving a very narrow turning at the top, so as not to thicken the waist-band. Turn the material from you, tack along the top. Now you have the material towards you, take a narrow turning and tack along to the other side of the webbing, leaving the turned-down edge of the material quite level with the webbing; this will be secured by sewing the skirt to it, Turn down one inch at each end, sew round and hem across. Now sew three hooks on the webbing side at the right hand end of the band, two quite at the end, and one in the centre of the band, three inches from the others. At the other end of the band, on the material side, sew one eye at the centre and two eyes three inches from the end.

Take the foundation skirt and fold in the middle of the front breadth. Three inches from the middle on each side take up a pleat 4 inches in length, ¾ inch wide at the top, and graduating to nothing at the bottom of the four inches. A similar pleat is required over each hip.

Cut down the placket-hole in the centre of back width, 13 inches long, hem it round. Next take the band, hook it into all the eyes, double from the centre between the hooks and eyes at the middle of the back, so that the ends of the band are exactly even; this will give you the exact middle of the band in front.

Take the foundation of skirt, turn down the ½ inch allowed for, and place the material side of band towards right side of skirt, pinning through both together; slightly full the skirt until you have passed over the hip pleats as far as the seam of back breadth. On the eye side of band fold what fullness you may have into a double or triple box pleat, leaving a piece at the back quite plain from inner to outer eye.

Return to the other side of front, sewing to band in the same way as described for the first side, with this exception that the box pleats are at the end of band from hook to hook.

Run the casings for steels on the inside of foundation; the lower casing 15 inches from the bottom, the entire width of back breadth. (The casings must be wide enough to run the steels in easily). The upper casing should be 10 inches higher. The steels should be bound at the ends with a piece of wash-leather or an old kid glove, and should be put into the casings and secured at the ends just before putting on the drapery.

The elastic and tapes for tying skirt back are best put on after the drapery. We will now state how;

At the ends of the casings five inches of elastic should be firmly sewn. To the loose ends of the elastic sew tape about fourteen inches long; this must be very strongly sewn to the elastic.

We will now give directions for trimming the foundation to the illustration shown on the front of this Supplement.

First, cut ten widths of the material, four and a half inches wide, join ; if the material has not a self-colored selvage, the selvage must be cut off and the edges must be over-sewn when joined, turn up and hem one edge by hand or machine; if by hand, the stitches must be almost invisible on the right side. Begin kilting from the hemmed edge, and pleat each width to a quarter of a yard.

Have a needleful of tacking cotton, and tack each pleat as you make it, being sure that all are equal in size; finish the bottom length. Next, tack a second line along the middle, arranging the plaats quite evenly, according to the grain of the material. Now take cotton the color of the material and tack the pleats along the top edge; this done, press with a hot iron ; if the material is thick and stubborn, damp it previous to ironing it. Turn down the top edge about half an inch, and tack it along with cotton of its color. This done, press the turn-down quite flat with a hot iron.

Your kilting is now ready for placing on the skirt; the hemmed edge should be one-eighth of an inch above the bottom of skirt. Sew the kilting on by hand.

For the box-pleated skirt, which has three tucks, cut five breadths forty-five inches long, and five breadths twenty-seven inches long ; join all the long lengths together, then all the short ones, and join the short to the long. Now turn up a hem all round three inches deep. If for machining, it must be be tacked ; if for hemming, pinning will be sufficient.

Take a piece of card five inches in depth, and make a mark on it three and a quarter inches from the bottom, put the bottom of the card to the bottom of the hem, turn the material to the exact depth of the card. Now tack your tuck to the three and a quarter inch mark on the card.

Now fix the second and third tucks by leaving one and a half inch, between each tuck, as only the stiches of the top tuck are shown in our illustration. You will easily keep your tucks even by cutting the card three inches deep, and marking it at one and a half inch. Place one edge of card at the tacking of the tuck below the one you are fixing, turn the tuck to the other edge of card. The tucks must now be stitched and pressed.

You must next double the five front breadths, putting in a pin to mark the middle of the front. The front middle pleat is twelve inches in width ; it takes rather more than one breadth for this pleat, as the folds must wrap over under the centre of pleat at back. Leave spaces of two inches each side of this pleat. The two side pleats measure ten inches each when finished ; they must be made in the same way as described for front pleats. The five back breadths must be pleated into three ten inch pleats, with spaces as before.

Now tack all these pleats, beginning at the hem, and tack the front breadths six times at regular intervals; for the back breadths four times will be sufficient. Press with a hot iron on the wrong side. After pressing keep the wrong side to you, and put two tapes across the pleats at the front breadths, sewing the tapes to the back of the pleats. You must not tighten the tapes, nor must you take the stitches through to the front of pleats. One tape is to go across the middle of the pleats, and one between this and the top of the breadths. The back pleating will not need tapes.

Next take the middle of front breadth of foundation and the middle of the front centre box-pleat; pin the pleating to the foundation centre to centre. The bottom of the hem must fall one inch over the kilting at the foot all round. Place the foundation and pleating on a table, and pin closely ; hold the skirt up, shake it, and see that it is even before stitching it to the foundation. When you are satisfied that it hangs evenly sew strongly.

For the front drapery, cut one breadth of the material twenty-two inches long, and two breadths each sixteen inches long ; join these three breadths together straight at the top, the long breadth in the middle. Slope the middle breadth at the bottom so that it graduates to the side breadths.

To put this drapery exactly in the proper curve run a tacking thread on the skirt, beginning at the side seam nine inches below the waist, and twenty inches below the waist in the centre of front. Look well at the illustration, and put the tacking line in the same slope as is shown in the illustration; both sides are alike at the bottom of front drapery. You will not find it necessary, for arranging the front and back drapery properly, to put the skirt either on a stand or on a person,

Fold the front drapery exactly in half, then pin it to the centre tacking-line and run it to the skirt, taking care not to tighten the drapery; sew both sides on and begin the pleating at the waist, first putting a mark in the centre of drapery. Pleat the whole of the right side of drapery into a number of small deep pleats and pin it to the foundation from the front to the seam of the back breadth.

Now arrange the left side of drapery, at about two inches from the front make five pleats close together about two inches deep. When this is pleated fasten it just below the waistband to the foundation, there will be a straight unpleated piece from these pleats to the seam of back breadth of foundation; now take the end of the drapery and pleat it up towards the waist. The drapery must fall quite loosely over the line it was tacked on at the bottom; sew the drapery strongly to the foundation just below the waistband, where it has been pined, and make it neat by hemming a piece of ribbon or binding over it. The sides will be made neat when placing the back drapery over them.

For the pocket, take a piece of the bodice-lining fifteen inches long and fourteen inches wide, double this lengthwise, turn over two corners together to form a triangle of six inches, cut them off, face up the slanted top of the pocket with a piece of the dress material, turn the faced side out and stitch down the short side and along the bottom, turn the pocket and stitch again about a quarter of an inch from the last stitching. Unpick the side seam of skirt, commencing ten inches below the waist, and pick out seven and a half inches of the seam. Turn the skirt inside out, sew in the pocket so that the facing shows on the right side of skirt. At the top of the pocket a piece of tape ten inches long must be sewn to it, and afterwards fastened to the waistband.

For the crinolette, divide the crinoline into three pieces, join them together, turn up a hem so that the crinolette will be fourteen inches deep, pleat in three double box-pleats, allowing the centre pleat a little larger than those at the sides, bind it along the top with a piece of tape, sew it to the inside of foundation-skirt just on the lowest steel casing, and sew it down the sides to the seam of skirt. Now sew on the tie-strings as before directed.

Take the three yards of material left for back drapery, cut in two, join and press the seam, turn under at each side at least three inches.

Pleat the drapery into a large triple box pleat wide enough to cover the back as far as the joints of the side drapery The middle of this box pleat must go exactly to the middle of the back, pin it there firmly On the left side sew the turn-down piece over the ends of the front drapery. Carry the pleat down 17 inches, turn under 8 inches, so that it forms a deep puff; sew this pleat under the puff to the skirt and slip-stitch the outer pleat an inch from the edge down to the skirt. The remainder of this side of the drapery must be turned under to form a second deep puff, which should terminate nine inches above the foot of the skirt. Now go to right side and loop it up in the same way, this will leave the centre hanging loose, which must be looped up and sewn to the skirt about 24 inches below the waist. wai t. Pleat the lower end of the drapery, turn it under, allowing it to fall three inches lower in the centre than at the sides; sew firmly to the skirt. This is dress complete. *See cut next page.*

COMPLETE DRESS CUT.

CUTTING AND MAKING FULL ROUND BAND BODICE.

Cut and piece the lining as directed for a pointed bodice, with the exception that you cut it only two inches below the waist all round. Tuck the bust-pleats, which have to be stitched in the lining only; put the side-pieces on to the back. Next put the two underside-pieces on to those next back, stitch all the seams, and press them. The seams of the lining for a full bodice, after being snipped, are turned towards the material; this prevents the need of over-sewing.

Put the lining upon the material, allowing fifteen inches from the edge of material to edge of the front lining; this is for the fulness. If you wish more fulness you must allow it here. Cut the material away to the lining at the armholes, the shoulders, and side. Tack across the shoulder, round the armhole, and down the side-seam, being sure to attend to the pierce holes. Place a pin here and there between the under arm-seam and first bust-pleat.

Now go to the throat. If you wish to have a pleated bodice commence about two inches from the shoulder, and pleat up all the material in small single or box pleats as preferred. When this is done, pleat at the waist, arranging the pleats to cover the two bust-pleat seams on each side. If you wish the fulness gathered, run a thread in a curved direction at the throat, commencing the same distance from the shoulder as you would for the pleats. Now draw up the gathering; see that it fits round to the pierced throat of lining, and if it should be too high or too low place another gathering above or below, as the case may be. At the waist gather three or four times, commencing from the second bust-pleat.

For the back, cut a piece of material twenty-four inches wide, and the length for the back ; fold it in half, and pin the lining of the back upon it, with the armhole side next selvage of material. Cut round as described for fronts, open out the lining and material, pleat or gather the material to the size of back of neck, and also at waist; when this is drawn up to the size required, lay the lining on the material and tack down the shoulder, round the armhole, and down the side. Now pin and tack the shoulder and side-piece together as directed for pointed bodice, put it on to see that it fits properly, correct the two sides as described for pointed bodice. When corrected stitch the backs to the front. When stitching do not join the side-seams next front below the waist. The fronts are turned down as described for pointed bodice, and the bottom is bound with ribbon or tape. The sleeves and collar are made and put on also as directed for pointed bodice.

TO MAKE THE MATTRESS OR IMPROVER.

Take a piece of bodice lining, and make a bag measuring nine inches across the bottom and seven inches across the top, seven inches deep ; leave the top unsewn, put in the horsehair and turn in the top and sew closely. To keep the horsehair in its place take a needle and thread and knot it at intervals quite through as a mattress is knotted, This is sewn to the eye side of band, putting the centre to centre of band ; put a hook on the loose side of improver and an eye on the band of skirt to fasten it to.

TO MAKE A DOUBLE CORDING FOR FACING A BASQUE.

Cut a piece of material on the cross three inches wide, take a cord and place it on the wrong side of material a quarter of an inch from the edge, turn the material down over the cord and tack it with a needle and cotton quite close to the cord for the required length, put a second cord half an inch from the first, fold the material back with the cord in it so that this second lies immediately above the first cord, and run on the tacking-line with silk or cotton the color of the material, tack through the material under both the lines of cord, so that they are firmly held together ; pull out the tacking, and stitch on the bottom of basque to directions already given.

Our readers may think that telling them how to make one dress is not teaching them dressmaking ; but the illustration we have selected gives kilting, box-pleating, tucking, and a drapery, which, though it looks simple, needs a good deal of careful management to make it set properly ; as all these trimmings are employed in various ways in different dresses, showing how to do them properly in this shows how to do them in any other arrangements, as the same principle will apply, though the kilts be wide and box-pleating narrow. We have told them how to make a pointed bodice and a bodice with full back and front. If a basque-bodice is required, the plan of cutting, fitting, and putting it together must be the same as for a plain bodice, leaving the additional lining and material at the bottom of bodice to form the basque.

MATERIALS.

VELVET AND VELVETEEN.

In cutting velvet great care must be taken so that it shades dark alike on looking from the top downwards; this can easily be ascertained by holding the velvet in the hand and looking selvage-way down it; one way it will shade lighter than the other. The pile of the velvet or velveteen feels rougher towards the hand when it is rightly placed, and should be brushed in the contrary direction to other materials; thus, you would brush a velvet bodice from the waist to the throat.

WOOLLEN MATERIALS.

If you cannot decide which is the right or wrong side of a twilled material, hold the selvage down, and see that the twill goes from right to left upwards.

Cashmeres are twilled only on one side, French merinos on both; they are each always folded right side out.

CRAPE.

It is not now usual to use crape double, it is lined with a soft black muslin; it is difficult to tell which is the right and wrong side of crape but if you observe closely, the small raised lumps are on the right side, but in holding the selvage to you when the crape is on the right, side the crimp slants from left to right.

ADVICE TO MARRIED LADIES.

Ladies who are stout or corpulent should never wear a basque or polonaise fastened below the waist line. The princess' dress and tight-fitting wrapper in one piece, is particularly unsuitable. The skirt should be lengthened at the top only, and made by the diagram of skirt No. 2, in this book. A dressy half-fitting basque or sacque made of either a bright or delicate tinted basket cloth, according to fancy, and trimmed with full ruches and jabots of creamy Oriental lace, or some such fluffy trimming from the neck to the waist, and then carried around both sides of basque, will be becoming and stylish. White aprons and ribbon bows at the waist line in front should be avoided. As all drapery at the back is now worn extremely full, wide whalebones can be run in the back breadths of skirt, to increase the bouffant effect where it is most desired.

The blending of colors requires good judgment and refinement, as well as knowledge. Custom and fashion govern many things, and colors are now put together which a few years ago would have been considered not only in very bad taste, but also exceedingly vulgar. For instance, pink and red, red and orange, green and blue, as well as purple and blue, although contrasting colors are frequently shaded one into the other, with great skill and charming effect. Rich warm colors blend well with those that are delicate and pale. As dark crimson or scarlet with pale blue or gray; pink with gray, white or black, and green with violet.

Those colors which form the greatest contrast to hair and complexion are considered the most becoming. Black and white are worn by all ladies, and considered in good taste for any one; but the first is not favorable to a very dark complexion, or the last for a very pale one. The rosiest complexion loses much of its freshness by coming in contact with the same color; light crimson and maroon are apt to cast a green shade over the face. A white fichu or ruching should be worn to separate the bright face from the brighter dress, and the effect will be charming. White is particularly becoming to a fresh complexion, as it relieves it of much color; but, on the contrary, those ladies who have the whole face tinted a deep reddish hue, particularly the nasal organ, should avoid white, unless separated from the skin in some manner by edging the draperies with black.

The material, color, make and fit of the dress may be as near perfection as possible, yet it is the trimming, lace around the neck, bosom and sleeves, the jewelry, ribbons and flowers, that gives the finishing touches that impart tone to a lady's costume. Sufficient attention is not paid to these details, or we would never see costly jewels worn with a common dress, and cheap lace on a royal velvet robe, either in the street, the market-places, or the fashionable reception room.

Then, too, care should be taken to suit the style of costume to the figure, as some goods impart height and others have the opposite effect. Stripes should not be worn by tall, slender persons, unless made crosswise. Broad plaids and large figured goods make a short person look dumpy; reverse these styles and you will do well.

It is unnecessary to describe the infant's robe, lady's night dress and low-necked yoke, as they are all cut on the same principle as the bathing robe. The yoke for a skirt may be cut any depth by laying the material on the diagram below waist line, as in skirt No. 2.

This system can never become old fashioned, as the measures are taken direct from the body, any change of style, such as longer or shorter shoulder, higher or lower dart, or looser sleeve, can be made at will. The diagram of plain basque is the key-note to the American Lady Tailor System, and when once mastered, any lady will be enabled to cut, without a pattern, every article of clothing worn by each member of her family from the youngest to the oldest. The rules are so few and so simple that any one with ordinary intelligence can learn them in a few hours. We invite criticism, and ask the world at large to test its merits.

WIDTHS OF MATERIALS.

						Inches.
Alpaca	.	.	.	.·	.	.	26, 34, 36
Beige	.	.	.	.	.	.	25, 28, —
Brocade	.	.	.	.	.	.·	22, — —
Broche (Woolen)	.	.	.	.	.	24, — —
Cashmere	.	.	.	.	.	.	46, — —
Cloth	.	.	.	.	.	.	38, 54, 60
Crape	.	.	.	.	.	.	23, 42, 60
Crepe de Chine	.	.	.	.	:	.	24, — —
Flannel, White	.	.	.	.	.	24 to 72
Flannel, Colored	.	.	.	.	.	26, 32, —
Foulard	.	.	.	.	.	24, — —
Grenadine	.	.	.	.	.	26, — —
Longcloth	.	.	.	.	.	28 to 54
Linen	.	.	.	.	.	28, 32, 36
Merino	.	.	.	.	.	45, 46, —
Nun's Veiling	.	.	.	.	.	25, 46, —
Paramaka	.	.	.	.	.	42, — —
Princess Dolman Cloth	.	.	.	.	52, — —
Silk, Black	.	.	.	.	.	22, 26, —
Silk, Trimming	.	.	.	.	.	18, 20, —
Satin	.	.	.	.	.	18, 27, —
Serge	.	.	.	.	.	25, 32, —
Surah	.	.	.	.	.	22, — —
Velvet	.	.	.	.	.	18, 20, —
Velveteen	.	.	.	.	.	27, 28, —
Washing Silk	.	.	.	.	.	21, — —
Zephyr	.	.	.	.	.	31, — —